THE EMOTIONAL INTELLIGENCE PRIMER

THE **EMOTIONAL INTELLIGENCE PRIMER**

How to Be the Difference

That Makes the Difference

for Today's Leaders

DR. DON R. BOOZ

First published by Booz and Associates

Copyright © 2017 by Don R. Booz

First Edition

donbooz@me.com

Cover Design: StyleMatters, LLC, info@style-matters.com

Interior Design: Jerry Dorris, StyleMatters, www.style-matters.com

Library of Congress Control Number: 2017912166

ISBN: 978-0-692-92556-0

This book is dedicated to all the nurses
who tirelessly serve in health care systems.
Thank you for being the difference
that makes the difference.

Table of Contents

Acknowledgements

I am so fortunate to have been surrounded by gifted mentors, teachers, and instructors who have guided, challenged, and motivated me by sharing their knowledge and wisdom. I am grateful for all of the ideas, advice, and encouragement that have helped me to be my best possible self.

I want to express my deep appreciation and gratitude to Lila Martin, Vice President, the University of Kansas Health System, who gave me the opportunity to instruct and work with the Perioperative managers and directors. Specifically, I wish to acknowledge and thank the Perioperative managers and directors. My thanks to Kathy VonWyl, Lanette Kelly, Lisa Elm, Tim Kistner, Jennifer Hertig, Greg Crawford, Eugenia Johnson, Sandy Turner, Melinda Loy, Anna Werner, Holly Grier, Laurie Hay, Michael Chenoweth, Sarah Villanueva, Brian Selig, Cindy Ladner, Nikki Anderson, Levi Rojas, Patty Gieger, ReGina Davis, Renee Walters, and Jenny Maddox, who are the difference that makes the difference.

I also want to thank my clients, both past and present, who make me a better coach with every interaction. In addition, I want to acknowledge and express my appreciation for my editor, Rachel Fending. And although there are too many people to mention, I continue to love and appreciate my two daughters, Amanda and

Colleen, numerous friends, and countless colleagues who have given me feedback and encouragement for my life's journey.

Most of all, I want to thank my wife and best friend, Cindy Brenize Booz, for her incredible support. This book would not have been written without her continued love and encouragement. Thank you, Cindy, for being an exceptional person who has made the difference in my life every day I draw breath.

Foreword

All of us want to know how to be better performers. But what is the difference between the top 10% and someone who's simply an average performer? What are the subtle yet effective strategies those exceptional performers use that the rest of us don't?

The key, as you'll learn in this book, is emotional intelligence. The simple definition of emotional intelligence, otherwise known as EQ, is the ability to understand and manage both yourself and others. Unlike your IQ, which is fixed, you can develop your EQ and become more emotionally intelligent by focusing on and practicing a set of competencies and behaviors.

Emotional intelligence not only has an intriguing outlook on performance that is easily understood; it is backed by years of solid, evidence-based research. One of the current gaps, though, is the "how to"—what to do, when, to raise your emotional intelligence. Now, Dr. Booz's *Emotional Intelligence Primer* fills this gap with solid and tangible tools and skills to help you attain top performance.

The concept of emotional intelligence has been with us since 1995, introduced by Dr. Daniel Goleman in his popular book *Emotional Intelligence*. It is now recognized as one of the fundamental building blocks of social psychology; a quick Internet search of *emotional intelligence* yields about 14,900,000 results.

We know today that emotional intelligence is the key factor that propels leaders to success, more so than technical expertise and IQ.

As a practitioner of emotional intelligence leadership since 2001, I know that what leaders do in the heat of the moment determines their effectiveness. Their output in terms of decisions, communications, and actions defines them as being the best. This strategic intelligence and ability to quickly read yourself, others, and the situation as relevant input will help you prevent errors and mistakes and enhance just the right actions. The magic all happens in those critical moments when the leader can be the hero—or the goat.

Dr. Booz's *Emotional Intelligence Primer* takes you on a tour of the top models, strategies, and tools to get you to this "best boss" destination. He is your tour guide and acts as a connoisseur of brain-based boosters. As a specialist, authority, enthusiast, and expert, Dr. Booz has the experience to give you the shortcuts, teaching you what to do, and when, to be an exceptional leader. He has the recipes already mastered; you just have to follow them and practice them. Dr. Booz breaks EQ down into a different recipe in each chapter, with homework to focus on for five days. One look at the cutting-edge topics in the Table of Contents will let you see that he has done the reading and research for you and gleaned the "top recipe ingredients" for you to consume and share with your teams.

Great leaders leave their team members feeling more capable and motivated. Team members walk away full of positive neurotransmitters that connect them to their boss and their coworkers. Dr. Booz's clients feel heard, honored, and helped by his emotional intelligence leadership. They refer to this as "getting Boozed." We know alcohol can act as a social lubricant by taking the edge off emotional situations. Dr. Booz, in his coaching style and the lessons he teaches in this book, affords you the skills and tactics to address challenges and develop your talent in effective and natural ways.

So read on and "get Boozed" to become a more effective leader using your emotional intelligence.

—**Relly Nadler, PsyD, MCC,**
author of *Leading With Emotional Intelligence:
Strategies for Building Confident and Collaborative
Star Performers* and *Leadership Keys Field Guide:
Emotional Intelligence Tools for Great Leadership*

Introduction

There comes a time in most people's professional life when they ask, "What am I doing, and is there a way that I can do it better?" This is such a time for you. You sought this book out because you've arrived at a place in your career where you're ready to move "to the next level"—to achieve even more, and make an even bigger difference in your organization. I wrote this book for you, for my clients—and for myself, really.

Every week I meet with leaders who are doing a fantastic job responding to the needs of their organization in a variety of situations. They are using their emotional intelligence, leading their employees to excel, and building strong relationships with clients and customers—but they've asked me to coach them because they want to be so much more.

Step into any bookstore, and you can find a truckload of books that attempt to teach you how to improve your work performance and be a better leader. Some I've read and discarded, because, let's be honest, after a while they tend to repeat each other. Yet by reading so many books, I have gained new insights and understanding about the world around me.

I have also learned a lot from my own mentors over the years. And, like you, I have learned from my failures and my successes. As a result, my map of the world has been greatly enlarged.

Each of us forms a unique map of the world based on our family background, education, life choices, and experiences. This is our personal road map, and it is responsible for how we experience and give meaning to particular events and situations. Our map of the world also determines the number of choices available to us. The bigger and more enriched our map is, the more options we have for dealing with life's challenges.

I have learned from all of the many experiences of my life, and my map has expanded accordingly. This book allows me to share not only what I know to be true, but what I have learned really works.

Experiencing all this book has to offer will require discipline and work on your part. You cannot just read; you must *do*. Some insights and exercises will come easily for you. Others may be not so simple to put into practice. Sometimes it's fine to put the book down and reflect on what the material means to you. Other times you will want to try out a new lesson by driving it around town and honking your horn so everyone can see the "new you."

The best way to read this book is to begin at the beginning and finish at the end, but it really doesn't matter. Whatever page you open to, you'll find a nugget of truth that can improve your day. What counts is your willingness to be reminded of what you already know and to learn things that you didn't know. My goal in writing this book is to help you be "the difference that makes the difference" at work, at home, and with everyone you meet.

You're already living a rich and productive life, but I know that you are capable of so much more. We all are. I believe that your best possible self is emerging every day you draw breath. So breathe. Read. Watch. Learn. The more you pay attention, especially to yourself, the more you will be that difference in the world. We need everything you can offer us to help make this a better place to be.

Thank you for reading, and thank you for becoming an emotionally intelligent leader.

CHAPTER 1

EMOTIONAL INTELLIGENCE

The Difference That Makes the Difference

The brain works in mysterious ways. Every day, researchers discover something new that gives us insight into the human mind. Neuroscientists are finding out more about the neurotransmitter system. We are learning about the production of serotonin, dopamine, oxytocin, and endorphins and their effects on our life.

Neuroscience and the study of neuroplasticity give us up-to-date information about how we can reprogram our mind.

That is the essence of emotional intelligence—reprogramming ourselves to be more proactive instead of emotional and reactive. Essentially, emotional intelligence is the ability to be self-aware of our emotions and to recognize, understand, and manage their influence on us. When we are more self-aware, we are also better able to self-regulate, because we recognize the emotional impact we have on those around us. The emotionally intelligent leader knows that effective leadership requires us to be more in tune with ourselves and thus more able to interact positively with others.

If you as a leader want to be your best possible self, it is helpful to become more aware of the choices available to you. When you do not fully understand your options, your unconscious programs will make choices for you. In other words, if leaders do not consciously determine their programs, their programs run them. Leaders who do not have a clear picture of their best possible self often make unclear choices when faced with important decisions. And because these critical decisions are often the difference that makes the difference, that's a problem.

As an executive coach, I fully understand that leaders are often too busy to add one more task to their already crowded schedule. As one of my clients said, "I only wish I could get into the habit of meditation, but I just don't have the time." Another client told me, "Asking me to keep a gratitude journal is just one more thing that I *should do* and don't have time to do."

This book is not about doing; it's about being. Emotional intelligence is about how you exist in the world. Yes, I work with my clients on how to incorporate journaling, meditation, focused breathing, exercise, and a good night's sleep into their regular daily life. Yes, I help them learn to navigate each and every day with a healthier perspective and a literally healthier mind and body. But with this book, I am offering a different, more tangible set of tactics for you to implement. You don't have to "add one more thing." You simply have to notice what you are already doing (and thinking) and tweak it.

My mission statement is, "Changing the world, one skill at a time." My desired outcome is to make a positive difference in the lives of my busy clients. I have found that organizations (no matter how big or small) spend a lot of time training leaders in what to do. What we *don't* teach leaders is how to think, how to look at the world with new choices and more options.

Not too long ago, a CEO client of mine, Linda, showed me her calendar and said, "Do you see next Wednesday at 2 p.m.? I have four meetings scheduled at the same time, and everyone attending those meetings wants me to be there." Then Linda confided, "I'm delighted when one of my meetings is canceled for the day." She went on to say, "I am often torn between which meeting is the most important for me to attend. There are days when the only thing I can do is hold it together."

I know Linda is not alone. You've probably felt the same way.

The focus of my work is to help leaders like Linda build the skills they need to do so much more than just "hold it together."

Every leader has meetings, quite often too many meetings to choose from. You're just one person—you might not be able to attend all of the meetings that are expected of you. Effective leadership is not just about meetings and time management, anyway. It's bigger and deeper than that.

You might be familiar with the notion that our energy flows where our attention goes. Where is your energy? Where is your attention?

To illustrate how important it is to pay attention to where you're focusing your energy, I often tell the story of the old Cherokee chief teaching his grandson about life—the story of the two wolves.

"A fight is going on inside me," the old chief said to the boy. "It is a terrible fight between two wolves. The first wolf is evil—he is anger, envy, sorrow, regret, greed, arrogance, self-pity, guilt, resentment, inferiority, lies, false pride, superiority, and ego. The second wolf is good—he is joy, peace, love, hope, serenity, humility, kindness, benevolence, empathy, generosity, truth, compassion, and faith. The same fight is going on inside you—and inside every other person, too."

The grandson thought about this for a minute, and then asked his grandfather, "Which wolf will win?"

A common version of the story ends with the old Cherokee chief simply saying, "The one you feed." However, it is rumored that in the Cherokee nation, the story ends this way:

The old Cherokee chief replied, "If you feed them right, they both win. You see, if I choose to feed only the second wolf, the first wolf will be hiding around every corner, waiting for me to become distracted or weak, and he'll jump to get the attention he craves. He will always be angry and always be fighting the other wolf.

"But if I acknowledge him, both wolves will be happy, and we all win. For the first wolf has many qualities—tenacity, courage, fearlessness, a strong will, and great strategic thinking—that I have need of at times and that the other wolf lacks. But the second wolf has compassion, caring, strength, and the ability to recognize what is in the best interest of all.

"You see, grandson, the first wolf needs the second wolf at his side. To feed only one would starve the other, and it would become uncontrollable. To feed and care for both means they will serve you well and do nothing that is not a part of something greater, something good, something of life. Feed them both and there will be no more internal struggle for your attention. And when there is no battle inside, you can listen to the voices of deeper knowing that will guide you in choosing what is right in every circumstance.

"Peace, my son, is the Cherokee mission in life. A man or a woman who has peace inside has everything. A man or a woman who is pulled apart by the war inside him or her has nothing. How you choose to interact with the opposing forces within you will determine your life. Starve one or the other, or guide them both."

As a leader, it is your goal to have peace within. To be at ease, professionally and personally. To know that you can give your best and not get burned out. That is the whole point of emotional intelligence. I've never met anyone who does not welcome more peace and less stress into their life. Let's get you on that path.

CHAPTER 2

GOOD LISTENING

The "Pay Attention and Notice" Game

The higher we travel in any organization, the more important it becomes that we embrace the critical truth that everyone has a different map of the world. Our map contains our ideas, thoughts, beliefs, and emotions, and it is constantly developing, expanding, and changing as we experience life.

Our family, friends, education, and life experiences all contribute to our map of the world and help us communicate it to others.

We are also guided by our own map when we speak and listen to others. Or, at least, we think we are listening.

People listen to each other for a variety of reasons. Sometimes we listen simply to obtain information. Other times we listen to learn about and better understand another person. Often, we listen for the chance to respond with what we know and what we want the other person to know. And still other times, we listen for pure enjoyment, because we like what we are hearing.

As a leader, you are already aware of the power of good listening. Yet sometimes, even the best listeners are too busy or too distracted to really hear what someone is saying. And there may be good reasons for not listening:

- We really don't have time to listen at that precise moment.
- We think the conversation can wait.
- We realize this is not the time or place to have the conversation.

Yet good listening is the most important aspect of being a leader. By becoming a better listener, you become a better leader.

Not too long ago, I entered a coaching relationship with a new client, Adam, at the request of his board chairperson. Adam knew that he was being coached because he had a listening problem. When I asked him to share his understanding of the situation, Adam politely told me, "I don't need to listen to people. I am the CEO—people need to listen to me."

Adam was not willing to listen to me, either, so our coaching relationship did not last long—and, unfortunately, neither did his career. His termination by the board could have been prevented if he had been willing to learn from coaching and practice better listening skills.

Good listening skills promote good relationships. However, many leaders do not know how to listen *effectively*. In 2006, researchers asked more than 1,400 leaders, managers, and executives to share their views of their most needed skills and their biggest mistakes.[1] The top three considerations were good communication, effective people management, and a sense of empathy and emotional intelligence. The most common mistakes were failure to provide appropriate feedback, failure to listen, and failure to use the appropriate leadership style.

Over the years, I have noticed various ways that leaders signal that they are not listening. Below are some of the most common signs.

Seven Common Ways to Be a Poor Listener

1. **Disinterested listening**—listening without eye contact, nods, or verbal responses.
2. **Preoccupied listening**—listening while greeting others as they walk by.
3. **Calculated listening**—listening to hear the perceived agenda or purpose for the conversation.

4. **Invalidated listening**—listening for a pause or any opening to negate, rebuke, criticize, or refute what the other person said.
5. **Distracted listening**—listening while looking at the computer screen or texting during the conversation.
6. **Assumed listening**—listening only for what we want to hear.
7. **Hijacked listening**—listening while interrupting and taking over the conversation.

So, what does good listening look like? More important, how do we know that we are listening? Below are seven important skill sets for listening with successful results.

Seven Important Skills to Be a Good Listener

1. **Paraphrase what you heard**—repeat what you thought you heard.

    Speaker: "I am dissatisfied with my work schedule, and I need to change it."

    Listener: "Let me make sure I understand you.

You don't like your work schedule, and you want to change it. Is that correct?"

2. **Give the "big picture" of what you heard**—restate what you heard into "bigger chunks."

    Speaker: "I am having problems with a coworker who thinks she knows more than anyone else. I have been working here a lot longer than she has, and besides, I know that she is cutting corners and not doing her job the way she is supposed to do it."

    Listener: "It sounds like you are having difficulties with a coworker who does not value your experience and knowledge."

3. **Ask questions about beliefs you heard**—ask clarifying questions to expand on beliefs.

    Speaker: "I will always be struggling, because life is so hard for me."

    Listener: "How would you know if that weren't true?" or "What would your life be like if you had no struggles?"

4. **Reframe what you heard**—interpret the details in a different way.

Speaker: "We seem to argue a lot."

Listener: "Yes, we have the ability to disagree. Maybe this also means that we want to hear other opinions besides our own."

5. **Reflect the feelings in what you heard**—respond with empathy and understanding.

    Speaker: "I want to transfer to another department, but I can't afford it."

    Listener: "I am really sorry. It sounds like you are feeling frustrated and trapped here?"

6. **Validate what you heard**—show you understand, and offer a way to change the thinking process.

    Speaker: "I am having lots of problems with time management."

    Listener: "Time management is not easy for everyone. If you had to teach me how to be better at time management, how would you do it?

7. **Offer a metaphor for what you heard**—accept what was said and offer a contrasting view with a different analogy.

    Speaker: "I miss the old forms, and I can't get used to the new way of doing things."

> *Listener:* "Yes, lots of people have the same thoughts. And it may take some time for us to drive the new forms around town while getting used to new brakes and a different steering wheel."

As you can see, listening is not something to add to your calendar or to-do list. It is something you are already doing—and something you can learn to improve on once you begin to pay attention and notice your own behavior and thinking.

To help boost your performance in the "pay attention and notice" game, each chapter in this book offers you a set of daily exercises. These questions are designed to help you become more self-aware, and that is the core of emotional intelligence. Don't just skim over them and keep reading. *Do* the exercises—every day. Use a journal or notebook to record your observations, so you can reflect on them later. The more you practice discipline in this regard, the more your emotional intelligence will grow.

Personal Inventory Exercise

Day 1

- Today, pay attention to *how* you listen. Can you determine whether you are a poor listener or a good listener?
- What did you notice?

Day 2

- Today, pay attention to the emotional and nonverbal responses of people during your conversations (e.g., body language, eye movement).
- What did you notice?

Day 3

- Today, listen to connect—that is, listen with the intention to really hear and understand what the other person is saying.
- What did you notice?

Day 4

- Today, reflect the feelings and emotions of the speaker.
- What did you notice?

Day 5

- Today, use a metaphor to capture what the speaker is saying, or reframe what you hear into a positive alternative way of seeing things.
- What did you notice?

TRY THIS

Over the course of several days, practice each of your new skills while listening (e.g., reframing, paraphrasing). Reflect on your experience, and analyze which method of listening is the most comfortable for you and which method seems to be most comfortable for the speaker. Then pay attention to what happens when you return to your "default" mode of listening.

CHAPTER 3

YOUR INNER VOICE

Supportive Companion
or Negative Critic?

I n Chapter 2, we discussed listening to others, the hallmark of being a good leader—but how well do you listen to *yourself*? Paying attention to your own inner voice is just as important, and maybe even more difficult.

We all talk to ourselves, even though we might not admit it to our family and friends. Psychologists describe the voice inside our head as our "self-talk" or "inner voice." Sometimes we might hear it as a voice from the past, like a parent or teacher. Other times our inner voice might not sound familiar—simply a voice we hear inside our head.

As a coach, I often hear people say that their inner voice speaks to them in the third person, and frequently is not very supportive: "Don, you idiot. Why did you say that?" Such a punitive inner voice seems to be the norm with most people.

Many leaders I've coached are frustrated by how emotionally draining their inner voice can be. One CEO told me that he is berated all day by an inner voice that keeps reminding him what he should and should not do. Another leader told me, "I can't get it to shut up and leave me alone." Still another executive said it this way: "Because of my inner voice, I am constantly second guessing my leadership. And no matter what I do, my inner voice lets me know that I should have done better."

To better understand the inner voice, you can ask yourself several questions:

- Whose voice is it? Do I recognize the inner voice as belonging to someone I know?
- Is my inner voice friendly? Helpful? Demeaning? Encouraging? Attacking?
- In what situations do I hear the inner voice most often? While I'm doing a task, in a conversation, or in a meeting?
- How does my inner voice make me feel?
- How do I respond to the inner voice: engage in dialogue, agree, or debate with it?

- What is the positive intention of my inner voice?
- What would I do or say if I did not have the inner voice?

These are important questions to ask, because quite often we simply accept the inner voice. We give it complete control over us, without first stopping to question the truth of what it tells us. When I asked a CEO I worked with what would happen if he told his inner voice to "shut up and go away," he responded, "I don't know, but I would probably miss the companionship."

Isn't that interesting? I was surprised that he considered such constant negativity to be companionable. What about you? Would you miss the constant chatter inside your head, even if it's not encouraging?

I have found that the inner voice usually follows a pattern. Many of us have a "parent–child" relationship with our inner voice. It treats us as if we were children, and its message is usually delivered in some sort of critical or berating manner. Would we talk to others the way we allow our inner voice to talk to us? Highly doubtful.

To better understand your inner voice, it is helpful to realize that the inner voice is not simply self-talk. Some experts describe the inner voice as a way of thinking. When we listen to it, we are having an inner dialogue that is outside the awareness of others (assuming, of course, that we are not talking out loud!). Yet sometimes we allow our inner voice to give us misinformation or negative messages about ourselves. And, what's worse, sometimes we believe it.

I have spent countless hours coaching people about how to counter all of the negative and misinformed messages their inner voice sends them. Sometimes it is only a matter of telling the inner voice to "shut up" or saying, "No, you are wrong." One client, James, found that by simply saying, "Delete," to the negative messages, he could make them go away. Another leader told her negative inner voice to take a permanent vacation.

Unfortunately, it is not always that simple; most often, the solution is more complex. For whatever reason, many people have lived with a negative and critical inner voice for so long that they cannot imagine another way of being.

I find that most of our inner voice's messages leave us with an attitude that is mercurial at best. The inner voice can be positive and affirming one minute and degrading or negative the next minute. Often, it doesn't even take a minute for the swing to take place. If we aren't careful, what we hear can become a belief statement about our leadership. And if we accept all of the negative messages as truth, we seriously weaken our success as a leader. Yet our inner voice can also be a positive resource and companion that helps us be the difference that makes the difference.

Below are seven helpful ways to embrace your inner voice as a positive resource and daily influence.

Seven Ways to Embrace Your Inner Voice

1. **Reprogram the inner voice.** Reprogram your inner voice by not allowing it to express negative and condescending messages (e.g., "I am smart and good at what I do").

2. **Become an editor.** Offer factual evidence about distorted information (e.g., "I got the position because of my skill set and not because of who I know").

3. **Offer a second opinion.** A second opinion is often helpful when what we hear doesn't match what we experience (e.g., "Although Joe might be upset with me right now, my staff appreciates that I am consistent").

4. **Preprogram the day before you leave for work.** Look ahead at the personal interactions of the day, and anticipate the positive (e.g., "Today I choose to see myself as being confident and self-assured").

5. **Only allow positive messages.** Listen to positive messages about your desired outcome (e.g., "I am at my best, and I can handle any situation").

6. **Keep a journal.** Recall past events or situations that affirm things you did well (e.g., "I had a great day handling staff and affirming their professionalism").

7. **Correct "always" and "never" statements.** Carefully listen and correct all universal statements (e.g., "I don't *always* interrupt people when they talk").

Personal Inventory Exercise

Day 1

- Today, pay attention to what you hear your inner voice saying about others.
- What did you hear?

Day 2

- Today, pay attention to what your inner voice is saying about *you.*
- What did you hear?

Day 3

- Today, listen for any negative "parenting" language from the inner voice.
- What did you hear?

Day 4

- Today, edit any negative messages, and allow yourself to debate any negative criticisms from your inner voice.
- What did you notice?

Day 5

- Today, hear yourself deliver only positive messages.
- What did you notice?

TRY THIS

Before you close your eyes at night, decide what kind of attitude or demeanor you want to project the following day. Allow yourself to visualize every interchange, meeting, or situation for the next day. Repeat the same visualization process as the first thing you do in the morning. The very last thing before you leave the house for the day, look at yourself in the mirror, and tell yourself the type of person you wish to be during the rest of the day.

CHAPTER 4

MULTIPLE MESSAGES

Reading Between the Lines

Emotional intelligence hinges on your self-awareness, your ability to read yourself and others, and your willingness to tune in better to your own emotions and those of the people around you. Honing your emotional intelligence takes some practice, but the rewards are exponential. Once you get used to tapping into your inner voice, you will be better equipped to dissect the external voices that are speaking to you. And what's more, you will begin to tune in to the "multiple messages" you're receiving.

We all send and hear multiple messages all day long. We hear multiple messages at home, at work, with friends and family members.

Once upon a time, my wife and I were watching TV. I got up to get myself a second glass of wine. As I poured, my wife asked, "Is there any more wine left?"

I responded, "Yes," took my glass, and sat back down next to her.

She looked at me in surprise and said, "I thought you were going to pour me some more wine."

I replied, "Well, you didn't ask me." And, of course, I immediately got up to get her some more wine. (You don't stay married for more than forty years without learning to take immediate action when you mess up!)

My wife's question—"Is there any more wine left?"—inferred multiple messages beyond her actual words. What she *said* was, "Is there any more wine left?" What she *meant* but did *not* say was, "Please pour me some more wine, too." By failing to listen to her inferred message, I risked my wife's irritation with me.

That "inference" is often referred to as "white space,"[1] and it is the real information, communicated but not verbalized, that we respond to in a relationship. Someone says something, and we respond not just to what was *spoken* but to what we heard *unspoken*—the meaning behind the words. The more you are able to hear the unspoken messages in what people say, the more effective you will be as a leader, a spouse, a parent, and a friend.

The word *intelligence* comes from the Latin for "entering through the lines." Whenever we interact with others, we use our emotional intelligence to "enter through the lines"—to read between the lines of people's words. Sometimes we mistakenly assume that people know what we mean. Sometimes *we* don't know what we mean, but the people we're speaking to seem to "get it" anyway. I like to respond to those who make a confusing statement by saying, "I think I followed where you drifted."

I believe that people seem to fill in the space where we "drifted" without a lot of thought. They read between the lines and make an assumption—either correctly or incorrectly—about what we actually meant. Sometimes, people "connect the dots" erroneously and put their personal spin on what we are saying. In either case, we can place ourselves in an awkward situation by assuming that we know all of the possible meanings embedded in the messages we send and the messages we receive. That's where emotional intelligence kicks in.

For example, if someone says, "I don't understand what the issue is; *everyone* uses their cell phones at work," the real message might be, "You are the only one who has a problem with cell phones." Another message could be, "Cell phones are not an issue . . . management is the issue." And yet another message could be, "Tell me why cell phones are a problem."

How we respond to multiple messages is a key skill set for how we manage and lead people. When we hear a multiple message, many of us respond by trying to interpret the "real" content of the message being sent. In other words, we guess! And we can often guess correctly, either because we know the person (and his or her agenda) or because we are good at reading between the lines and connecting the dots. If that doesn't work, we try to decode the person's nonverbal behavior to guess at the intended message. However, watching and listening to someone speak does not guarantee successful communication—that is, real message sent and real message received.

Noam Chomsky, an American linguist and cognitive scientist, assumes that there are two levels of communication between and among people:

- *Surface structure*—everything that we say.
- *Deep structure*—everything others assume about the underlying meaning of what we say.

According to Chomsky, "The deep structure of a sentence is submitted to the semantic component for semantic interpretation, and its surface structure enters the phonological component and undergoes phonetic interpretation."[2] Therefore, the closer we can align what we say with what we want to say, the more coherent and articulate our communication will be.

We need to keep in mind that everyone tends to speak in generalizations, deletions, and distortions. This sometimes results in a form of mind reading, because we assume what someone else is trying to communicate. Yet what do we know about assumptions? They are not always correct. The brain simply cannot process all of the information available to it. As soon as our attention is focused on one place, our conscious mind misses large amounts of the rest of the world around us. Subsequently, we tend to speak and listen from these deletions, distortions, and generalizations.

Deletion is the process by which we selectively pay attention to certain portions of our experience while excluding other portions of that experience. For example, we can filter our own voice (what we are willing to share), or we can filter out someone else's voice (what we are willing to listen to). Perhaps your spouse or a close friend has accused you of "selective listening," or hearing only what you want to hear. We all do it, intentionally and not.

Distortion is the process that allows us to make shifts in our experiences with others; it often functions as a way to create or transform information. For example, if you receive a compliment from a coworker, you might interpret her words as a signal that she must want something from you. Most of the time, compliments are sincere, but we can distort them, depending on our state of mind and the situation at hand.

Generalization is the process by which one piece of a person's individual experience becomes enlarged to represent a whole category. For example, someone who was once robbed by a homeless person might translate that experience into a belief that "all homeless people are ready to rob me." Or you might make a general statement that you don't trust any teenager who wears his jeans so low they're practically down at his knees.

You can see how our map of the world affects our ability to properly filter multiple messages. But with your new awareness, as an emotionally intelligent leader, you will be able to bridge this gap more of the time. When you are the message's sender, being clear about what you want to say and how you want to say it helps to avoid miscommunication. When you are the receiver, asking clarifying questions is the perfect way to get past the "surface" level and fully understand what the deep structure might be.

How Leaders Can Avoid Sending Multiple Messages

There are several keys to successful communication, but most important, as a leader, you want to know two things:

- How do I avoid sending multiple messages?
- How do I respond to multiple messages?

Emotional intelligence always begins with self-awareness. So, to be even better communicators, let's begin with ourselves before we explore how to respond to others.

Before a meeting or an important conversation, you can clarify your thoughts and root out any unintended multiple messages by taking a series of steps:

- Be clear about the content you want to send. Ask yourself, "What is it I want to say, and what is the 'takeaway' I want people to understand?"
- Fill in any gaps by asking, "What am I missing?" and, "What else do I need to communicate?"
- Imagine what the "smartest person in the room" might ask or take away from the meeting.

- Ask yourself, "Is there any way that my content can be misinterpreted?"
- Take about five minutes to preprogram yourself—planning out what you will say and how you will say it.
- See yourself delivering what you want to say by visualizing where you will stand or sit, plus how you will use gestures or other nonverbal behaviors.
- Take time to truly prepare by rehearsing what you want to say. It's helpful to hear yourself deliver the message, either silently in your head or out loud.

At the end of the meeting or conversation, take a moment to make sure your message came across as you intended:

- Ask whether there are any clarifying questions.
- After listening to a question, repeat and paraphrase what the person said, correcting any assumptions or misinterpretations.
- Clarify any misperceptions or misunderstandings.
- Be ready to restate and interpret the "takeaways" from the meeting or conversation.

How Leaders Can Respond to Multiple Messages

You can plan your words ahead of time to ensure that you don't inadvertently send multiple messages, but the odds are, you're still going to receive them from others. Knowing how to respond in the moment is key.

- Ask clarifying questions, such as the following:
  - "I am not sure I understand what you are trying to say. Could you restate your question?" (Note: This approach allows you extra time to formulate your response.)
  - "Are you also saying _____ ?"
  - "Help me to understand your question."
  - "Is there something I am missing in your question?"
  - "If I heard you correctly, you [paraphrase and restate question]?"

- Pay attention to generalizations, distortions, and deletions. Look for signal words, such as *always, all, never, should,* and *everyone,* and respond using clarifying questions:
  - "Always? Never? Has there ever been a time when _____?"
  - "According to whom?"
  - "How do you know?"
  - "Who specifically are you talking about?"
  - "Which people specifically?"
  - "In what way do you think _____ needs to happen?"
  - "Who was talking to whom?"
  - "What are you asking me to do?"
  - "In what way are you suggesting _____?"

- Repeat the question (paraphrase), so people know you heard them and to let them hear themselves think and speak.
- Manage your internal dialogue by silencing the voice that wants to disrespect or silence the person speaking.
- Remember to breathe, and take deep breaths as often as possible.

Questions stay with us until and unless they are answered. Often, our questions have a greater influence on our relationships than our statements do. Accordingly, the questions we ask are important for helping us improve our relationships with others. The bottom line is this: The better we become at asking questions and paraphrasing, the better able we are to connect with others.

The best way to understand what people are really saying is to practice the art of asking clarifying questions. Below are some guidelines for how *not* to ask questions and for how to ask advanced questions.

How *Not* to Ask Questions

Use a "why" question only if you can't think of a better phrasing. When you ask, "Why?" you're telling people to explain themselves, to justify their actions or their reasons for doing or saying something. A "why" question is the easiest way to put someone on the defensive. It is more helpful to begin with "what" or "how" questions. It feels different to be asked, "How did you decide to do that?" versus "Why did you do that?"

Refrain from using "Don't you think?" and "Do you think?" questions. When we ask "Don't you think _____?" or "Do you think_____?" questions, we are really telling someone what *we* think. We're not really asking a question but giving an opinion or statement disguised as a question. Similarly, when someone asks you this kind of question, translate the content of the disguised question into an opinion or statement of the other person.

Limit "What do you want me to do?" questions. Many people know what they don't want to do or have happen. However, few people can state what outcome they *want* to see happen. More important, other people are often glad when we take on the problem for them. Asking people what they want to do invites them to think and "own" their situation. Asking, "What do you want to do?" often has a different outcome than asking, "What do you want me to do?"

How to Ask Advanced Questions

Ask reflective questions—to help people think, instead of giving advice.

- "What _____ will make the most difference for you?"
- "How do you want others to _____?"
- "Can you envision yourself _____?"

Ask challenging questions—to help people explore various options available to them at the time.

- "How will you know if _____ is successful?"

- "What will you do if _____ happens?"
- "How will you feel if _____ doesn't happen?"

Ask problem-solving questions—to help people create a "well-formed" outcome.

- "Are there steps we have missed or that we need to discuss further?"
- "What is the positive outcome you want?"
- "What fears or hopes do you have for _____ ?"

Ask motivating questions—to help people commit to a plan of action.

- "How will you celebrate when _____ happens?"
- "What would you do if you really believed in yourself?"
- "What if you chose not to act this way, what would life be like?"

Ask affirming questions—to help people feel good about their decisions, relationships, and work circumstances.

- "What are some of the positive things you learned about _____ ?"
- "What can you do that almost no one else can do?
- "What do you want your legacy with this company to be?"

Ask reframing questions—to help people see a different perspective or adopt another person's point of view.

- "What is the positive intention of _____?"

- "How do you think _____ is feeling right now?"
- "What steps could you take to change how people perceive you?"

Ask ecological questions—to help people look at the big picture and understand the impact on the systems around them.

- "How will _____ affect your personal life, work relationships, work hours, free time, etc.?"
- "Do you feel any 'pushback' from _____ when you do_____?"
- "How do you interpret _____?"

Personal Inventory Exercise

Day 1

- Today, notice the various multiple messages you encounter—at work, from your family, on TV, and elsewhere.
- What did you notice?

Day 2

- Today, when you speak with people, listen for their possible intended message and the multiple messages. Then observe which messages people respond to when you talk to them.
- What did you discover?

Day 3

- Today, become more self-aware of the multiple messages you send during the day.
- What multiple messages did you hear yourself conveying?

Day 4

- Today, when you listen to people speak, pay attention to their generalizations, distortions, and deletions. Then ask clarifying questions.
- What did you observe from the reactions of the speaker?

Day 5

- Today, respond in conversations by always beginning with a question.
- What did you notice?

TRY THIS

While watching and observing others, listen to which message they respond to the most—surface-structure or deep-structure content. Then pay attention to how often people use generalizations, distortions, and deletions. In your leadership role, ask others how they know what a speaker is really saying. If possible, teach others what you have learned about multiple messages. Explain how to ask and how *not* to ask questions.

CHAPTER 5

EMPLOYEE MOTIVATION

The Inner Work Life

Listening. Communication. Emotions. What is the connecting link? These are all essential building blocks of emotional intelligence. As a leader, if you are striving to make a difference in your workplace, you need to start by paying attention to what you pay attention to.

Among other things, increased employee motivation is a direct result of improving your own emotional intelligence. It's well worth the effort, because a desire to motivate employees is a recurring theme for leaders everywhere. A Google search for "How to motivate employees" yielded more than 45,600,000 links. The search results displayed such titles as these:

- *Thirty-Seven Ideas for Motivating . . .*
- *Ten Tips to Help Motivate . . .*
- *Twenty-Four Proven Ways to Motivate . . .*
- *Three Easy Steps to Motivate . . .*

Apparently, there are a lot of theories about what motivates employees to do what we want them to, but is there a key that unlocks the "motivation door" every time? One manager recently told me that what motivates employees is more a matter of luck than anything else. Yet many of us spend an inordinate amount of time and energy trying to figure out the "tipping points" to nudge our employees up to the next level of performance. Do they need more money, more time off, more responsibility, or maybe a new title?

Most leaders tend to use two basic motivation strategies on a rotating basis: the "carrot" and the "stick." Both have proven to be somewhat successful for decades of management. Many leaders prefer the carrot method, trying to motivate their employees by offering money, recognition, food, gift cards, thank-you notes, and other novelty items. Sooner or later, they might find something that works.

A manager once told me, "If all else fails, there is always the 'happy hour' approach." But there always is at least one employee who responds, "Why did the company spend their money on this stuff? I would rather have a verbal 'thank you' once in a while."

Another employee might say to her colleague, "What I would really enjoy is for management to tell me I can leave work early today." There is no one-size-fits-all reward system.

The other motivation strategy—the stick—has been used for eons as well. As one leader told me, "If worse comes to worst, we cannot overlook the impact of punishment as a motivator." In my experience, most leaders prefer using the carrot instead of the stick—yet I've heard more and more managers stating that none of the carrots seems to be working anymore. One leader told me, "I have exhausted all of the tricks in my bag."

The above strategies for motivating employees can and often do work, but do they simply create more and more Pavlov's dogs in the workplace? Are we conditioning people to salivate for rewards just to be motivated to do their job? And if that doesn't work, will we pull out the big stick of punishment?

Leaders are always looking for employees who enjoy coming to work and who are fully absorbed in their job. Managers, leaders, supervisors, and CEOs often spend a lot of extra time and effort trying to get and keep people motivated.

Almost without exception, the leaders I meet with lament the same two struggles:

- Finding the right person
- Retaining the right person.

They know that finding the right person is only half of the equation. The hardest part is training and retaining the right person for the position. One leader I worked with, Marcus, told me that even after he thinks he's chosen the right candidate, there are no guarantees about how long that person will remain on the job. Marcus said, "We spend a lot of time training and getting people up to speed, only to find out they aren't really motivated to do the work."

I am continually asked, "How do I motivate these people to do their job?" Research has shown that people are motivated by a variety of reasons. Dan Ariely, in his book *Predictably Irrational*, asserted that motivation dies when employees don't feel a sense of progress.[1] When we feel we are making a contribution to something, we perform better.

Daniel Pink looked at the bigger picture and the apparent paradox of motivation.[2] According to Pink, three things motivate people:

- Control over their work
- A desire to be better at what they do
- The chance to be part of something bigger than they are.

Perhaps the most compelling evidence for what motivates people was offered by Teresa Amabile and Steven Kramer.[3] After rigorously analyzing 12,000 daily journal entries provided by 238 employees in seven companies, Amabile and Kramer found that people need to sense that they are contributing something worthwhile and that their contributions are both noticed and valued. The authors wrote, in their book *The Progress Principle*, that "if we believe that our work is valuable and we are successful, then we feel good about this key part of our lives. If our work lacks value or we feel we have failed at it, then our lives are greatly diminished."[4] Their research results present a convincing case for paying closer attention to the inner emotional life of your employees—or, as Amabile and Kramer put it, their "inner work life."

A person's inner work life is a system made up of his or her perceptions and thoughts, emotions and feelings, and motivation and drive. According to Amabile and Kramer's research, performance improves when workers have positive perceptions of their job, emotions about their job, and motivation to do their work. By paying closer attention to what motivates employees, leaders can better predict the ultimate success of the organization.

After sifting through 12,000 daily journal entries, Amabile and Kramer found predictable triggers (events) that can inflate or deflate motivation. They described these triggers as contributing to *progress* or *setbacks*. The progress journal entries were described as catalysts or nourishers; the setback journal entries were described as inhibitors or toxins.

The key to motivating employees is to support their progress in meaningful work—that is, to focus on the nourishers. For example, constantly changing direction and making adjustments to strategy does not help employees to feel valued, but following a consistent course with clear purposes and outcomes adds value and meaning to employees' work.

But just how, exactly, can we support our employees in doing meaningful work? Sometimes it is as simple as helping a colleague to complete a task or letting people know that what they said or did was important. The small actions and the little gestures can create the most positive impact on motivation.

Of course, it does not take a rocket scientist to figure out that doing meaningful work can produce positive emotions and that doing tedious and irrelevant work has the potential to generate not-so-good emotions. Likewise, progress can produce positive emotions, and setbacks can elicit negative emotions. Most leaders are aware that everyone responds differently, and what is motivating to one employee might be demeaning to another. Yet the research clearly shows that the key to motivating employees is to pay attention to how we treat them and whether they can see the significance of what they do.

The research in *The Progress Principle* reinforces the importance of emotional intelligence in the workplace. Those 12,000 journal entries expressed the silent emotions of employees that leaders seldom hear verbally communicated. Because they know that everyone has emotions (expressed or not) and that employees want their work to matter, emotionally intelligent leaders will produce the greatest employee satisfaction and retention in the workplace.

Personal Inventory Exercise

Day 1

- Today, notice what employees say about the workplace.
- What did you hear?

Day 2

- Today, identify any "toxins" that might be present in the workplace.
- What did you notice?

Day 3

- Today, notice whether there is any confusion among your employees about desired outcomes and goals for meaningful work. In other words, what do you notice about their ability or inability to solve problems?
- What did you notice?

Day 4

- Today, express appreciation for a team member's "small" but positive behavior.
- What did you share, and what was the reaction?

Day 5

- Today, support a coworker by verbally and publicly recognizing his or her positive contribution to the team in a team meeting.
- What did you say, and what was the reaction?

TRY THIS

Self-awareness is the cornerstone of emotional intelligence. Without self-awareness, leaders cannot adequately lead a team. At the end of each day, spend some time reflecting on how you supported and encouraged team members. Ask yourself whether you sufficiently recognized positive contributions or discouraged a team in any way. What did you notice about your behavior, and how do you think your behavior affected the team?

CHAPTER 6

BOUNDARIES

If You Don't Set Them, Someone Else Will

One of my favorite movies is *Pirates of the Caribbean: The Curse of the Black Pearl.* In one scene, Elizabeth, having been taken hostage aboard the *Black Pearl,* uses the pirate's medallion to influence Captain Barbossa to return her to shore. When the captain ignores her request, Elizabeth shouts, "You have to take me to shore! According to the Code of the Order of the Brethren."

Captain Barbossa laughs and sharply replies, "First, your return to shore was not part of our negotiations nor our agreement, so I must do nothing. And secondly, you must be a pirate for the pirate's code to apply, and you're not. And thirdly, the code is more what you'd call 'guidelines' than actual rules."[1]

Captain Barbossa is correct . . . there is a difference between an actual rule and a guideline. Similarly, there is a difference between a boundary and a guideline. Although most of us know the difference between a rule and a guideline, we may confuse boundaries and guidelines. A boundary is something that indicates a hard limit, a line that must not be crossed. A guideline, by contrast, simply sets conditions for our future behavior.

Depending on the work context, both words (*boundary* and *guideline*) can mean the same thing. And, in many cases, the two tend to get confused in both interpretation and impact. Not too long ago, a leader told me that he didn't know he had crossed a boundary by dating his administrative assistant. In his words, "I knew that dating her could be problematic for some people, but I didn't see anything written in our employee handbook about employee dating relationships." He believed that since he had checked the handbook for information about dating employees and found nothing, he was in the clear. He didn't realize there was an implicit boundary around dating a direct report.

Most institutions have their own set of rules and guidelines—either spoken or unspoken, formal or informal, written or unwritten. Most rules are put into writing, and when someone breaks a rule, it can be the reason for termination.

Yet we all know of leaders who don't enforce the rules. And when that happens, eventually we begin to hear people ask, "Why have rules in the first place?" It is a good question to ask when we see a rule being interpreted as "more what you'd call a guideline."

In many work environments, boundaries—or the things we absolutely cannot do—are codified in an employee manual. More often than not, our profession and work position tell us what is acceptable and not acceptable behavior in the workplace. However, the distinction gets complicated when we see people interpreting rules as guidelines and guidelines as boundaries.

The ramifications are even more complex when we consider that the distinction between boundaries and guidelines is more or less left to our personal interpretation. For some people, guidelines and boundaries are essentially the same. I see both serving the same purpose—they help inform us about what is appropriate or inappropriate behavior.

When we don't set boundaries, we allow others to tell us what is appropriate or inappropriate. Without clear boundaries, we might not even recognize how our behavior can be detrimental to our work and personal relationships. It is important to define what a healthy boundary is and recognize where we need to set some guidelines in our professional and personal life.

What Is a Healthy Boundary?

Someone once told me that the most important and healthiest boundary is knowing where I end and another person begins. Dr.

Murray Bowen, a 20th-century clinician at Georgetown Medical School, called this process *differentiation*.[2] According to Bowen, differentiation is more a direction in life than a state of being: the ability to strike a healthy balance between interpersonal connection and independent action. Emotionally mature leaders know how to set boundaries in their interactions with others by exercising their individual choices and holding themselves back from emotional fusion with others.

Simply translated, differentiation means having a good sense about appropriate levels of interaction. Differentiation is being clear about our goals and values, both inside and outside the workplace. As one leader said, "I never go out drinking with my staff after work, because I want to keep my boundaries clear. I never want my staff to think that I am their best friend and that they can share inappropriate information with me." Reading through your professional code of conduct for information about appropriate boundaries is a good place to start the process of differentiation.

We can expand our understanding of healthy boundaries by looking at what boundaries already exist at our workplace. Quite often, they are written into a code of conduct or ethical standards for acceptable behavior. It is also helpful to know whether a particular boundary only applies when you are on the job. Is there a boundary about socializing with coworkers outside the workplace? If you keep your phone tucked away during the workday, is it okay to text a friend while eating lunch at your desk?

Finally, how are the boundaries in your life enforced, both on the job and away from the workplace? Below are some helpful guidelines for creating, setting and keeping healthy boundaries.

Typical Boundary Violations

- **Broken confidences:** Sharing information that is confidential and not meant to be shared without the knowledge or consent of the person or organization where the content originated.
- **Policy violations:** Disregarding established rules and policies. These policies are most likely written and include expectations for ethical behavior and code of conduct.
- **Secret meetings:** Enlisting or attending secret meetings without consideration of personal or professional vulnerability.
- **Personal needs:** Ignoring the responsibility to inquire about another person's interests, needs, and wishes.

Where We Need to Set Boundaries

Basically, there are two types of boundaries: those set at the workplace, and the more personal boundaries outside of work. Because you likely spend most of your time in the workplace, you'll probably find that your ability to set and keep boundaries is most frequently tested while you're on the job.

Workplace boundaries can be formal or informal. For example, you probably have already established several boundaries, whether you realize it or not. You've decided how many hours in a day you will work. You might have a boundary established around which positions you are willing to work or what you will and will not do while on the job. Consequently, your personal and professional limits tell you what boundaries you will set, and where you will set them.

Informal boundaries are best established as soon as possible, instead of after the fact. An informal boundary is simply a statement of personal preference. For example, when a colleague is sharing inappropriate information with you, it is best to tell him or her right away that you don't want to hear that type of information (boundary). If you wait a week or more after the conversation to share your informal boundary, your colleague might be confused and even upset that you didn't state your boundary earlier. He or she might even want to know why you have such a boundary.

I have found that sometimes we only get one shot at setting boundaries in the workplace. For example, it is often easier to set a boundary when we first start a position, rather than after we have been in the position for a longer period of time. For that reason, it's best to have a clear sense of your boundaries ahead of time.

What Impacts Do Our Boundaries Have?

Most of us know the impact of our boundaries after they have been violated or crossed. Yet few of us like to express our dismay, except when we are pushed to share why we are upset. We may even ruminate for hours or days about when and how a boundary was crossed. Maya Angelou is often quoted as saying, "When you know better, you do better." Her words can apply to both how we set boundaries and how we respond after a boundary has been crossed.

People often make assumptions about our boundaries according to our actions. For example, when we listen to gossip, people can assume that gossiping about others does not cross any of our boundaries. It can be tempting, however, to adhere to our boundaries only when we are at the workplace.

For example, even if you are careful not to overshare at work, if you fail to establish clear boundaries outside the workplace, you might find yourself at an after-work happy hour, complaining about your latest fight with your spouse. Or you might not have clear boundaries when using social media (e.g., you wrote that "Wine Wednesday" Facebook post to make your friends laugh, but you forgot that your boss follows you on Facebook, too). In other words, you might share very personal and confidential information without regard to the possible negative consequences.

In the examples above, there is no perceived violation of a boundary, because there was not an established boundary about what is appropriate or inappropriate behavior. The consequence, however, can ultimately be termination from our job. If we fail to enforce healthy personal and professional boundaries, we send the message that people do not need to respect our boundaries. At the very least, people might not want to trust us with confidential information.

Emotional intelligence is about self-management through self-awareness. A more technical way of saying it is that emotional intelligence requires an internal locus of control, rather than an external locus of control provided by others. In other words, emotionally intelligent people (with an internal locus of control) believe that they are responsible for managing their emotions, whereas people with a strong external locus of control tend to blame or praise others for their emotions.

We set boundaries every day, or we allow someone else to set them for us. Sometimes these boundaries are weak or semipermeable, while other times, they appear to be rigid. Not too long ago, I was talking with a CEO, Nan, who said, "I know my boundaries and when I need to step in and suggest another way of doing things." Nan went on to say, "Boundaries are important around here. I don't go out drinking on Fridays, because I want my staff to know that I don't blur the lines between my role and their roles. I am not their friend, nor should I be."

Another CEO, Martin, stated it this way: "When I first took this position, I had to be very clear about how I was going to handle what was my responsibility versus what needed to be applied to others. I don't want to create a codependency on my leadership. I want my staff to think and create solutions to problems while informing me about their progress. From the outset, I told my staff,

'Feel free to bring me your problems, but never bring me a problem without a solution you want to try.' And I think my staff will tell you that I do just that, and I do not micromanage."

Emotional intelligence is about being aware of and managing our emotions in a variety of settings. Our self-awareness often requires us to set limits or boundaries for what kinds of relationships we need for our leadership position. This often requires us, as leaders, to make choices and to be very intentional about the best way to set clear boundaries. Most important, setting boundaries clarifies our responsibilities and roles with others. And setting boundaries requires practice, because it is not often taught in leadership training classes. Leaders with high emotional intelligence maintain clear boundaries for what matters most in their position. One of my clients said to me, "The best thing you taught me is to ask whose problem is it and what they want to do to fix it."

Seven Guidelines for Healthy Boundaries

1. **Be clear about your personal and professional values and goals.** Ask yourself, "What am I trying to accomplish by setting this boundary?"

2. **Decide what boundary needs to be set.** Ask yourself, "What is appropriate behavior in this context?"

3. **Realize that setting a boundary is not always easy.** Ask yourself, "What will happen if I set a healthy boundary?" and, "What will happen if I don't set a healthy boundary?"

4. **Be consistent with boundaries.** Ask yourself, "Am I consistent in setting and implementing my boundaries?"

5. **Recognize that boundaries will be violated.** Ask yourself, "What must I do to reestablish the boundary that has been violated?"

6. **Take responsibility for your professional position.** Ask yourself, "What do my position and profession expect of me with respect to when and where to set boundaries?"

7. **Preprogram yourself for disapproval.** Ask yourself, "How will I respond when people do not honor or respect my boundary?"

Personal Inventory Exercise

Day 1

- Today, notice how people express their professional boundaries.
- What did you notice?

Day 2

- Today, listen for personal boundaries that people express as personal preferences. If possible, inquire about the positive intention behind the boundary.
- What did you discover?

Day 3

- Today, become self-aware of your professional boundaries and how you express them to coworkers.
- What did you see or hear yourself sharing?

Day 4

- Today, allow yourself to express at least one personal boundary that is appropriate for the situation. Then watch and listen for any positive or negative reactions.
- What did you share, and what was the reaction?

Day 5

- Today, look for any professional boundary violations— either that others share with you or that you personally observe.
- What did you find out?

TRY THIS

While watching and observing others, notice how people respond to both formal and informal boundaries. Pay particular attention to how boundaries change with any given situation or person. Did people act confused, delighted, or dismayed when they encountered a boundary? How did their reaction match the boundary being expressed? Was the reaction appropriate? In what manner was the reaction expressed?

CHAPTER 7

TRIANGLES

An Emotional Coping Mechanism

As a leader, you are the emotional thermostat for your workplace, and you set the temperature for how people will act toward, interact with, and react to each other. We'll talk more about this in Chapter 9, but the connection can be obvious: If the leaders in a family or organization are anxious and frightened about their future, most likely the rest of the group will embody a similar type of anxiety.

Most healthy organizations are interconnected by an emotional force that somehow takes on the character of the most mature leaders. Conversely, most unhealthy organizations tend to organize themselves around the most dependent and most dysfunctional leaders. Rarely do people rise above the level of emotional maturity of their leaders. At some level, we all know that we have an emotional impact on each other by the way we exchange relevant information (both formal and informal). And, within each organization, this emotional reaction can be activated by a variety of events.

In his book *Failure of Nerve*, Edwin Friedman outlines how a well-defined leadership style is dependent on the emotional system of the organization.[1] He asserts that being a well-defined leader entails being differentiated—that is, being clear about our goals and values, both inside and outside the workplace, and striking a healthy balance between our interpersonal relationships and our own independence. And this differentiation rests solely on the capacity to know your personal boundaries and values. Friedman defines it as having "a non-anxious presence in the face of anxious others" and "containing one's reactivity to the reactivity of others, which includes the ability to avoid being polarized."[2]

Whenever people are anxious, they tend to share their anxiety with someone else. Dr. Murray Bowen was one of the first to theorize that people form "triangles" when responding to anxiety in a relationship.[3] Later, Friedman and several others agreed that anxiety is the driving force for creating emotional triangles.

Emotional triangles are formed when two people are anxious about another person or a group of people (e.g., the administration). They are typically a result of the initial and ongoing emotional energy that comes from the "unknowns," fears, and projected change in the organization. Quite often, the anxiety is the result of the actions and decisions of the organization. The more anxiety there is in the organization, the more likely it is that people will draw in a third person or a group of people to help defuse and lessen the anxiety.

Triangling others can be a strategy to help bond people against a common enemy, so to speak (e.g., "The bosses don't know what they are doing"). Triangles can also be formed to keep people out (e.g., "It's a secret, so don't tell anyone, but more people will be laid off in the near future").

On a daily basis, we influence each other by our emotions, both at home and at work. Not too long ago, a client told me she could tell what kind of mood her boss was in from the moment he walked through the door. In my client's words, "When I saw his face, I knew that I could not ask for time off on that day." She promptly shared this same information with the rest of the staff, just in case anyone else wanted a favor from the boss (i.e., she drew her coworkers in as the third point in the triangle).

It should be noted that not all emotional triangles are bad. Triangles can be an effective strategy for management. In fact, without triangling, many leaders would not be able to do their job. Or, at least, they could not perform as effectively.

One leader I coached, Larry, described his CEO as all knowing. "Nothing gets by her, and she knows everything that happens here," he said. "Claire is all knowing."

Larry was both amazed by and in awe of the CEO's "extraordinary" skills. What Larry did not know is that Claire received her information as the result of the many triangles formed within the organization. She was able to use those triangles to do her job better, as a benefit of the fact that the organization was functioning at a healthy level.

Any leader can use triangles to perform at a higher level. The first step is to recognize triangles in your organization and to be aware of how they are being used. It is also helpful to remember that anxious people increase the anxiety in the organization by triangling others.

One can be triangled into another person's anxiety without realizing it. Below are seven helpful tips for how to extract yourself from anxiety triangles you might find yourself enmeshed in.

Seven Helpful Tips for How to "De-Triangle"

1. **Recognize when you've become "triangled."** We are almost always in a triangle of one kind or another. However, recognizing our responsibility in the management of triangles is the key to being a successful

leader. As leaders, we are not ultimately responsible for the emotional relationships between and among employees. We are, however, required to be self-differentiated. Subsequently, the process of "de-triangling" begins with the self-awareness and self-management of the leader.

2. **Avoid that "special" feeling.** It is hard to resist feeling that we have been pulled into a triangle because we are so special or important. And sometimes triangles help us to know what is going on around us, so we are better equipped to lead. Sometimes, though, we simply want to know because we don't want to be left out. At other times, what we know grants us a certain amount of prestige and importance, which can be tempting. To guard against being pulled into unhealthy triangles, it is helpful for us to "own" our needs, wants, and desire for specialness.

3. **Remember that change often produces anxiety.** It's important to bear in mind that any change can and quite often does increase the anxiety in an organization. People's emotions can easily be triggered by a disruption in the homeostasis of the organization. By staying in contact with all employees and by using clear communication, you can reduce "thought

viruses" and lower the emotional thermostat to a more manageable level.

4. **Speak to both sides of the triangle.** The fastest way to de-triangle is to speak directly to all parties involved. Keep in contact with all parties, and gather information as appropriate. Pay attention to innuendos, gossip, and multiple messages. Realize that we can only influence the part of the triangle that we have a relationship with.

5. **Listen without condemnation.** Listen carefully to all sides of the triangle. Be aware of groupthink and thought viruses. Gather information by asking clarifying questions. Realize that the intensity of the expressed anxiety might not match the reality of the situation. Therefore, practice responding without overreacting.

6. **Maintain objectivity.** Treat all sides of the triangle as equals, and allow time for people to process information. Respond to concerns in real time and as quickly as possible. Analyze whether the situation matches the intensity of the anxiety. And, most important, keep confidences without contributing to further triangles by sharing inappropriate and confidential information.

7. **Figure out what "triggered" the anxiety.** Often, the "heaviness" of our information dictates whether we want to triangle others. In other words, the information we have might be too heavy for us not to share (e.g., someone is going through a rough divorce). In most cases, after the source of the anxiety is discovered, the emotional system tends to relax.

Personal Inventory Exercise

Day 1

- Today, pay attention to how often people share "news" about other people. Is it positive news or "news of concern"?
- What did you notice?

Day 2

- Today, listen for the emotions behind people's words. Determine whether the person sharing the information is upset, depressed, angry, dismayed, or happy about the information.
- What did you notice?

Day 3

* Today, if possible, see or hear how often the same news is repeated to others and to you. How has the information changed from one telling to another? Has the emotional content remained the same or intensified?
* What did you see or hear?

Day 4

* Today, pay attention to "thought viruses" and any erroneous information connected to a triangle. What conversation tells you that the triangle is being formed by misinformation?
* What did you notice?

Day 5

* Today, listen for anything that can tell you about who is being triangled—who is included, and who is left out. Can you find the source of the triangle and the possible positive intention behind the triangle?
* What did you find out?

TRY THIS

With every conversation you have, listen for the possible positive intention behind the anxiety. Notice how people react when you ask clarifying questions. You might also want to ask what the other person expects you to do with the information. It might be helpful to let the person know that you will check the facts and get back to him or her as soon as possible.

CHAPTER 8

THE AMYGDALA HIJACK

Preparing for the Tornado

Not too long ago, I was watching satellite TV, and the picture went black. Then words appeared on the screen: "Running receiver self-check." This was followed by another black screen and the words, "Step 1 of 2—Checking satellite settings—This will take a few minutes." I waited patiently, then saw, "A few more minutes to complete." I sighed, and got up to grab a snack. When I sat back down, the screen read, "Step 2 of 2—Receiving satellite information," with a percentage-complete bar steadily inching toward 100%. Within a short amount of time, my TV was back in action.

Sound familiar? Although many of us want to keep our emotions under control, it is no secret that sometimes we need to check our settings. (And emotional intelligence is all about running the self-check regularly.) We also need to rebuild our responses, because we all have emotions that can get out of control.

Sometimes our emotions squirt out in the most inappropriate manner and at the most inopportune moment. The reasons for an emotional outburst vary from person to person and situation to situation. We might have an emotional reaction in one situation but not show any emotional display in a similar situation a few days later. Or, at least, no outward display of emotion that the casual observer could easily recognize.

Neuroscientists tell us that the main culprit for most of our intense emotional reactions is the amygdala. The prefrontal cortex of the brain is the rational manager of our emotions, helping us to regulate and control them. The amygdala, however, can be described as the trigger-happy bandit of our emotions. When we feel something, the amygdala almost instantly causes an expression of that emotion. The amygdala assigns emotional meaning to our everyday experiences and provides the "fight or flight or freeze" response to threats we encounter in the world around us.

The amygdala monitors our emotions and motivates us to emotionally respond to whatever is around us. Our responses could be good, bad, or ugly—the amygdala doesn't discriminate. We have all observed people responding badly to unfortunate situations (and, let's face it, occasionally responded badly ourselves). Most of us have also witnessed (or participated in) the highly recognizable ugly response known as an "amygdala hijack."

The amygdala hijack—a term first coined by Daniel Goleman, the author of *Emotional Intelligence*—is, essentially, an emotional tornado.[1] Your amygdala grabs the controls, and without the prefrontal cortex as manager, your emotions come squirting out. The fallout from an amygdala hijack is similar to the aftermath of a tornado, too. Your emotions are so out of control that you don't know who or what relationship will be destroyed.

The amygdala hijack can be triggered at almost any time and place. And because the amygdala is hardwired to react so quickly, a hijack can happen quicker than you can say, "Oops!"

Some people describe an amygdala hijack as temporarily losing ten to fifteen IQ points. One of my clients put it this way: "Sometimes it feels like I have lost the ability to think. And until I was coached, I was constantly telling people that I was sorry for what came out of my mouth before I could stop it." Another leader said, "I usually do okay keeping my emotions in check. But when I get upset, people will immediately see the shadow side of me."

When we aren't distressed, the prefrontal cortex keeps our emotions relatively under control. Accordingly, an amygdala hijack is less likely to happen. Although the brain circuitry is very complicated, essentially what the prefrontal cortex does is similar to pouring water on a fire. Unfortunately, some of us use a garden hose when what we really need is a fire hose. And when someone is in the middle of an amygdala hijack, the best—and sometimes only—helpful response is to wait it out until the person has the ability to calm down.

By the time the amygdala hijack is over, most of the observers have "anchored" a picture in their mind about what they saw, what they heard, and how they felt at the time. To survive an amygdala hijack and retain any sense of leadership effectiveness, use the READ method (based on tornado preparedness guidelines) to recognize the signs and respond accordingly.

Steps to Managing an Emotional Hijack: READ

Recognize: The "Tornado Watch"

Recognizing the signs of an impending amygdala hijack is like going on tornado watch—you notice the possibility, and you heighten your awareness. A strong physical or emotional reaction to a situation is a good signal that a hijack might be imminent. The first step to managing your emotions is to get in the habit of recognizing when conditions are right for an amygdala hijack.

Physical conditions: Pay attention to what is happening to you physically. Is your body tense? Is your heart beating faster? Is your face flushed? Is your jaw rigid? Is your stance akimbo (hands on hips)? What is going on with your body? How are others responding to your nonverbal messages?

Emotional conditions: Pay attention to the sound of your voice and to the inner voice in your mind. Is it louder? Speaking faster? Is your "self-talk" saying things that you cannot verbalize? Are you unable to think clearly? Do you feel an impulse to lash out and let the chips fall where they may?

If you're seeing some of these signs, it's time to escalate to the next level.

Evaluate: The "Tornado Warning"

Once you've recognized the threat of a hijack, evaluating what emotion is being expressed is the first step to calming the amygdala. It is always helpful to name our emotions in order to tame them. Neurologists agree that simply giving a label to the emotion you're feeling makes an amygdala hijack less likely to happen.[2]

To defuse the impending explosion, it is helpful to do two things:

- Give voice to the emotion (e.g., "I am angry").
- Name the emotion's effect (e.g., "When you _____, I want to run away").

Assess: The "Tornado Damage" Assessment

We can only assess the damage of an amygdala hijack after we have had a moment to calm down. Although it is sometimes hard to recognize, thinking about the positive intention behind the actions that triggered you will help to calm the amygdala. In other words, every action has a positive intention. At some level, all behavior is intended or was developed for some positive purpose.

True, a positive intention can have negative aspects. For example, if you tell yourself, "I can never change the way I am," you might have the positive intention to prevent any false hope of reaching a goal or to avoid being further embarrassed by failing to exhibit consistent change. The result, though, is that you hold yourself back and deny yourself the opportunity to grow.

A person who smokes might have the positive intention of feeling more relaxed when he or she has a cigarette. Another person might subconsciously get fired from a job in order to be "forced" to find a better job or follow a dream. Some people might lose their temper (have a temper tantrum) in order to control others who might be fearful of them. By looking for the positive intentions, we may be able to express empathy while preventing another possible amygdala hijack.

Understanding the positive intention behind actions that angered or upset you is a hard mental exercise. The payoff is worth it, though. By recognizing the positive intention, you can disso-ciate (detach from the expressed emotion) and reconsider your actions and behaviors without getting involved (again) with the emotions that caused the tornado.

Decide: The "Tornado Clean-Up" Process

We all have choices. We make a decision about how to respond to every event or situation. And sometimes we have hard choices to make. In the aftermath of an amygdala hijack, the first decision is to ask, "What part did I play in this event?" The second is to decide, "What am I going to do about it?"

Given the variety of choices available to us, the best process to make any decision is to ask what are called the Cartesian questions:

- "What will happen if I do X?"
- "What won't happen if I do X?"
- "What will happen if I don't do X?"
- "What won't happen if I don't do X?"

Asking the Cartesian questions opens us to new possibilities for answers that are not yet a part of our awareness. When we combine this approach with the READ method, we are better equipped to manage any hijacks by the amygdala.

The READ method is a flexible tool, and we don't have to follow it exactly as outlined to unlock effective leadership. What is important is how self-aware we are when emotions begin to affect us. We can alter our future actions by being conscious of what triggers us. At the end of the day, the key is preprogramming ourselves for the next person, the next encounter, the next meeting, or whatever comes next on our screens.

Personal Inventory Exercise

Day 1

- Today, watch for any warning signs that indicate a potential amygdala hijack is about to happen, to yourself or someone else.
- What physical or emotional conditions did you notice?

Day 2

- Today, pay attention to your emotions, and name them as they happen during the day.
- What emotions did you name? What was the result of naming the emotions?

Day 3

- Today, pay attention to the behavior and actions of those around you.
- What do you think might be the positive intentions behind their behavior? What did you notice?

Day 4

- Today, be mindful of the many choices available for any decision you need to make. Say to yourself, "I am deciding to _____," before taking action.
- What did you find out? How did "voicing the choice" make a difference to how you felt?

Day 5

- Today, incorporate the Cartesian questions into your decision-making process.
- What did you notice about your confidence in making the decision?

TRY THIS

Whenever possible, use the READ method to process events and situations that are upsetting. Go deeper by deciding what specific action or behavior of the other person might have triggered an emotional reaction in you. If possible, recall when and with whom you had a similar reaction. Replay the scene, and ask yourself what choices are available to you now that were not available then. Then decide what the best course of action is to help restore the current relationship now. However, be aware that someone who is constantly upset with you and others might have deeper issues that require professional help.

CHAPTER 9

THE EMOTIONAL THERMOSTAT

Setting the Temperature for Your Organization

Leaders are the moral compass of any organization. Or at least, they should be. Leaders are also the emotional thermostat of any organization, department, or unit.[1]

Research clearly demonstrates that a leader's emotional intelligence has a direct impact on the emotions of the workplace.[2] This means that leaders set the emotional tone, and coworkers tend to take their cue from the leader's emotions. In the words of Edwin Friedman, "People rarely rise above the [emotional] maturity of their leaders."[3] Thus, a leader's emotional self-awareness is crucial.

Not too long ago, a new client, Fred, told me, "I don't consider myself to be an emotional thermostat; I am more like an emotional wreck trying to make it day by day." When I asked what exactly that meant, Fred replied, "It means that all day long I am responding to staff issues and the demands of the administration. My emotions tend to be all over the place." When I inquired further about how the staff might feel, Fred shrugged and said, "They just know that is how I am."

Perhaps. But that is not how it has to be. The more a leader tunes in to his or her own emotions, the more the workplace can be stabilized. We all know that dealing with people can be frustrating and exhausting at times. We also know that emotional intelligence can be the difference that makes the difference in effective leadership. Where does one start the process of becoming an emotionally intelligent leader? How do you ensure that you are the emotional thermostat for your team or organization?

In one of my favorite TED talks, Amy Cuddy argues that our body language actually shapes who we are.[4] Cuddy explains that we can change our self-perceptions simply by changing our body posture. She demonstrates the "power posing" of putting our hands on our hips (think Wonder Woman) or thrusting our arms up in the air. Being aware that our body language is shaping us can be a good starting place for better emotional self-awareness and control.

In addition to using power posing, Cuddy suggests that another starting point is telling ourselves that we are going to "fake it until we become it." I consider Cuddy's advice to be part of the preprogramming process that helps leaders avoid being hijacked by the emotions of others. When you are the emotional thermostat, you are the one who controls the temperature of the room.

Emotions are contagious. In the same way that we can catch the flu, we can "catch" emotions from others. To test this statement, smile at someone you don't know, and see how the person responds. My guess is that he or she will smile back.

This simple experiment illustrates how easy it is to catch the emotions of others. Some researchers describe this phenomenon as our "mirror neurons" responding to a visual cue.[5] I think that our emotional responses are much deeper. Many of us can easily detect when someone is emotionally upset, even before the person speaks. As one leader told me, "As soon as I enter the work area, I immediately pick up on the mood of the staff."

However, some leaders have an underdeveloped capacity to detect the emotions of others. One gentleman put it this way: "I rarely pick up the emotions of others unless they are either crying or physically fighting in front of me."

Most of us have experienced (in ourselves or others) an amygdala hijack, a situation when emotions are literally out of control. We can probably tell stories about how easily someone changed the entire tone of a meeting by his or her body language, tone of voice, or verbal message. In other words, the room's emotional thermostat can be set by anyone—quite often, by someone who might be unaware of what he or she is doing.

As leaders, we need to be conscious of this. We need to find the right balance between telling people how to act appropriately and coaching people about appropriate and inappropriate behavior. One leader I worked with simply stated, "I would rather tell people what behavior we will and will not tolerate. It gets the message delivered quicker." Yes, but being a dictator is not exercising emotional intelligence. There is not just one way to deliver a message.

The effective leader sets the minimum and maximum bandwidth of emotional expression. An emotionally intelligent leader knows when to appropriately express his or her own emotions and how to helpfully respond to the emotions of others. Being the organization's emotional thermostat encompasses the ability to communicate, understand, and express our emotions to others. The process of resetting the emotional thermostat begins when we monitor our own emotions and those of the people around us.

Below are seven helpful ways to reset the emotional thermostat.

Seven Ways to Reset the Emotional Thermostat

1. **Pay attention to triggers and hijacks.** In general, stop and listen more to the interactions of staff. What are you (and others) learning about staff interactions? If needed, take control and reset the emotional thermostat by stating, "There seems to be a lot of energy around _____. I am going to write that down, and we can deal with _____ on [date] when we have more time."

2. **Monitor emotions.** First, do a self-assessment of your emotions. Second, learn what others might be feeling and thinking. Ask, "I am feeling _____. Is anyone else having a similar feeling?"

3. **Notice patterns of behavior.** Does the person interrupt, speak loudly, or disrupt conversations? Are sarcasm, putdowns, or negative comments part of the staff person's repertoire? Ask, "Are we all interpreting the same information in the same way? I am curious to hear how some of the rest of you are feeling or what you are thinking."

4. **Identify any lingering positive intentions.** Identify any unspoken positive intentions for the negative behaviors of staff. Ask, "How can we have an even greater

positive impact in the days, weeks, or months ahead?"
"What are some other ideas that could be helpful?"

5. **Ask clarifying questions.** Dig deeper at the root causes by asking open-ended questions. Focus on understanding the group's perspective. Ask, "It sounds like this was not the most productive meeting of the year. How can we make it better?" "What are we missing?"

6. **Analyze the ecology of the department or unit.** Check out the positive and negative impacts of meetings, decisions, and staff interactions. Individually follow up with staff by saying, "I want to hear what you are feeling about our meeting."

7. **Reset the emotional thermostat.** Reset the emotional thermostat by acknowledging and anchoring the desired behavior whenever possible. State, "I just want to say how much I appreciate the cooperative spirit you all showed by working together on _____ last week."

You can reset the thermostat any time. Samuel coached with me to improve his confidence in his leadership abilities. At first he balked at the notion of emotional intelligence and "being the emotional thermostat." When Mandy was transferred to his department, however, Samuel became acutely aware that someone *always* sets the emotional thermostat. He also learned that it is up to the leader to set the dial where healthy and positive interaction can take place.

When Mandy first joined the team, she was outspoken about what she saw wrong and how to fix it. Mandy often hijacked Samuel's meetings by interrupting and trying to demonstrate that she was the smartest person in the room. She was also very negative and sent multiple messages (e.g., "I can't imagine anyone believing you when you tell people how good our product is").

Prior to coaching, Samuel dressed in a casual manner, and he never sat at the head of the conference table. With the help of coaching, Samuel started to dress in a manner that matched other executives in the company. He changed his seat to the end of the table, and he started to use hand gestures that were wider and more visually inclusive. Before each meeting, Samuel sent out an agenda, with a clearly stated purpose and desired outcome for every item.

Whenever Mandy tried to hijack a meeting, Samuel reminded her and the others about the purpose and desired outcome for the meeting. He also asked others to share their opinions by asking clarifying questions about their ideas. Mandy started to ask follow-up questions of her coworkers about their ideas. In fact, Mandy never hijacked another meeting. Samuel began to keep a leadership journal to self-reflect on his daily interactions while discovering how important his leadership was to the emotional thermostat of his department.

It cannot be stated enough: Self-awareness is the gateway to emotional intelligence. That is the point of the personal inventory exercises at the end of each chapter, and the point of the entire book. Take the time to pay attention to your actions, thoughts, and behaviors. Know that with every step you take, you are becoming a more emotionally intelligent leader and, thus, a more effective and successful leader.

Personal Inventory Exercise

Day 1

- Today, pay attention to which person sets the emotional thermostat at your workplace. (Note that the person may change from moment to moment or from day to day.)
- What did you notice?

Day 2

- Today, pay attention to how the emotional thermostat is set or reset (e.g., voice tone, body language, or verbal messages).
- What did you see, hear, or feel?

Day 3

- Today, notice how people respond to your nonverbal leadership style (e.g., eye contact, smiles, physical proximity, gestures).
- What did you notice?

Day 4

- Today, pay attention to how people respond to your verbal leadership style.
- What did you see, hear, or feel?

Day 5

- Today, notice whether, when, and how you are able to reset the emotional thermostat at your workplace.
- What did you notice?

TRY THIS

Over the next two weeks, focus your attention on any group issues or problems you might be facing. Decide ahead of time what your desired outcome is for each meeting. If and when someone hijacks the meeting, make eye contact, pay close attention to his or her body language, and paraphrase his or her statements. Then ask the person to explain his or her positive intention. For example, "I want to understand and not misinterpret your statements. Could you tell us again about your idea and how it fits into our decision, goal, and purpose for this meeting—our desired outcome?" Start keeping a leadership journal for self-reflection.

CHAPTER 10

MEETINGS . . . MEETINGS . . . MEETINGS

Making Them Productive

As a leader, your calendar is probably filled with meetings. Some are productive, and some are a total waste of time. Both formal and informal, scheduled and spontaneous, focused and scattered—"Too many meetings!" is the mantra of today's world. As one CEO told me, "I sit in meetings all day long, and I have the butt to show for it."

Never is emotional intelligence a more useful skill than when you are contemplating meetings and managing your schedule and your sanity. This chapter is an overall primer in meetings in general as well as part of the emotional intelligence primer, because meetings likely are a large portion of your life. After reading this chapter and completing the exercises, you will be able to watch your emotional intelligence grow as you interact in future meetings.

Sometimes you know ahead of time what a meeting is about and who will be in attendance. Yet, too often, you don't know much about the meeting other than that you are expected to be in attendance. Often, a meeting invitation is given without notice (e.g., "I am double booked, and I need you to be my representative at a meeting that is starting in thirty minutes"). Whether it is intended or not, the multiple message is, "What I need you to do is more important than what you currently have planned." (Aren't you glad you know about multiple messages now?)

Subsequently, you might attend the meeting without knowing why you are there and what the desired outcome is supposed to be. Yet it is part of your job, and you go because someone told you to be there. My coaching experiences have taught me that many leaders attend meetings with an attitude of "I would rather be someplace else." Other people at the meeting can observe this attitude within a matter of seconds by a plethora of micro-expressions and overt body language. I recently shadowed a coaching client who was totally unaware of her constant sighing and facial expressions that said, "Get me out of here."

But let's be honest. We have all attended meetings with an

attitude of not wanting to be there. And it often shows! The question is, "What can you do about it?"

Often, your decision isn't whether to attend the meeting, it's what you are going to do before, during, and after the meeting. A little emotional intelligence can be the difference that makes the difference in how you approach the many meetings on your agenda.

Before the Meeting: Set the Intention

Quite often, we don't give much thought about a meeting beforehand. We might not even know why we need to be there. We simply show up. And most people don't take the time to think about how they are going to be seen or how they want to be seen by those in attendance. Although we have no control over how people see us, we do have control over how we see ourselves. This control is called self-awareness.

Our self-awareness sets our intention for how we want to project our self-image to our peers, bosses, and colleagues. It begins even before the meeting starts. For example, how am I dressed? Where do I want to sit at the meeting? How am I going to sit throughout the meeting—how will I hold my hands, should I make eye contact, will I smile? Is there at least one positive contribution I can make while at the meeting? What positive affirmation can I give to those in attendance? What is the desired outcome? What can I contribute that is positive and helpful to move the agenda forward while meeting our desired outcome? And what can I say or do to be supportive of the facilitator before, during, and after the meeting?

These questions are the basis for "setting the intention" as you begin to think about the meeting. They provide a framework and an opportunity for visualization to help you prepare for almost any meeting. More important, setting the positive intention for the meeting provides for a better outcome. As one CEO told me, "Simply asking the questions and thinking about our desired outcome has allowed me to be more aware during the meeting." Another leader put it this way: "We tend to drift away from our agenda with tangents and divergent thinking. By helping to keep our focus on the desired outcome, setting intentions ahead of time has shortened our meeting time, and we are more productive."

Checklist for Setting Your Intentions for a Meeting

- Think of how you want to dress for the meeting (e.g., formal or more casual?).
- Think about where you want to sit and the way you want to sit during the meeting.
- Think about what you can contribute to the agenda that is helpful and affirming.
- Think about the desired outcome and how you can be supportive.

But what if you are in charge of the meeting? It's still necessary to set a positive intention, whether you are a participant or a facilitator of the meeting. However, as the facilitator, your role is to ensure that all participants clearly understand when the meeting starts and ends, the purpose of the meeting, and the desired outcome of the meeting. It is also helpful if participants understand why they were asked to be in attendance for the meeting.

One of the most important questions to consider before the meeting is the agenda. Neuroscience research tells us that employee engagement is higher when there is certainty about what is going to happen.[1] Subsequently, even the presence of an agenda beforehand helps to increase trust and the likelihood of reaching the desired outcome.

But an agenda is worthless if the facilitator does not follow it. One executive told me that she used to ask for an agenda before meetings, but since no one ever followed it, she stopped asking. Another agency created a policy that stated how long every meeting was to last and that if there was no agenda, participants were not expected to attend. When I asked about the success of the policy, my client described it this way: "I think it is still a policy, but after about a week, no one followed it."

In my experience both as a facilitator and as an attendee, the meeting agenda is important. However, it is not as important as a clear understanding of the desired outcome from the meeting. In other words, what is the meeting supposed to produce? Is it a written document, a verbal understanding, or simply information that needs to be shared? Being clear about the meeting attendees, the meeting agenda, and the desired outcome paves the way for greater success.

Checklist for Organizing a Meeting

- What is the purpose of the meeting?
- Who needs to attend the meeting?
- What is the desired outcome of the meeting?
- What agenda items will satisfy the desired outcome?
- What supporting documents do participants need before the meeting?
- What are the time frame and the location for the meeting?
- Who will facilitate the meeting?
- Who will take the minutes at the meeting?
- What are my self-awareness and positive intention for the meeting?

During the Meeting: Being Present

Like you, I have participated in a lot of meetings. Actually, to say I "participated" could be a stretch of the truth. To say I have *attended* a lot of meetings might be a more honest statement.

According to the National Center for Biotechnology Information, people tend to check in and out of conversations about every eight seconds.[2] Sometimes it doesn't take much for us to check out of a meeting. This is especially true if the meeting is boring or we would rather be somewhere else. We might be distracted by a ping from our cell phone or simply by seeing it light up with a new alert.

Many leaders now require all cell phones to be muted and put away during meetings. A CEO I know asks meeting participants to place their phones face down on the table. Both requests are good advice, yet they don't stop people from mentally checking out, thinking about what to make for dinner, what they would rather be doing, or the report they still need to write.

Being present in a meeting can take a lot of energy, so setting an intention to be present at a meeting is just as important as setting an intention before the meeting. If you attend a meeting just to attend the meeting, there is a good chance that others in the room will be able to tell that you don't want to be there. Instead, imagine that someone is videotaping you from the time you sit down until the time the meeting ends. Your body language and participation will be drastically different. And if you knew that you would be asked to grade your participation, your behavior would be different, too.

To practice being more present at meetings, set an intention to ask at least one clarifying question or state something positive about what someone else shared. A friend of mine likes to imagine that he will be asked after every meeting, "Did you do your best to be fully engaged and contribute something positive?" I teach my clients to paraphrase as much as possible during a meeting in order to stay engaged and to ask clarifying questions whenever they need to.

How to Prepare for the Worst-Case Scenario

When the "Smartest Person in the Room" Is Present

There is a "smartest person in the room" present at almost every meeting—the kind of person who has all the answers, knows just how things should be done, and isn't shy about saying so. When you find yourself coping with a person like this, you have at least two options. One option is to join the person, and the second is to redirect the conversation:

- "I agree with you about _____. And I also believe that we can accomplish [our task] by [restate purpose or resources for desired outcome]."
- "I agree with _____, and I would add _____."
- "It makes sense from your perspective, and I can only imagine how this _____ feels to you. Please allow me to share more information about [desired outcome]."

When the Meeting Has Been Hijacked

When a meeting has been hijacked, it often takes a little practice and finesse to get it back on track. Using affirmations to establish agreement is a good way to move forward without putting down the person's comments:

- "The concern you raise is the same concern I have about _____, and I appreciate you bringing this up. What we now know is [additional supporting resources and information for desired outcome]."
- "We will need to hold that concern until [date], because I don't have that information yet."
- "That issue is something we will want to discuss soon. Right now we want to [restate the purpose for this meeting]."

When Someone Is Dominating the Meeting

Sometimes a person who is "self-appointed" decides to speak for the group. This person has heard others raise concerns and has decided to give voice to what he or she has heard while speaking for no one in particular. One way to gain perspective (if not composure) in such a situation is to ask others in the group whether they are feeling or thinking the same thing. Most often, at least one person in the meeting disagrees with what has been stated. The trick is give that person enough support to share what he or she is thinking:

- "I am wondering whether anyone else has a similar concern?"
- "How do the rest of you feel about _____?"
- "We have heard from [name], and it would be helpful to hear how others of you view _____."

To show support, be sure to look people in the eye, especially if you see someone about to speak.

When Someone Questions the Direction of the Meeting

When a meeting starts to heat up, paraphrasing is often the most effective way to calm things down. Therefore, it is important to begin a paraphrase by matching the strength, speed, and tone of the speaker. Then you can "lead the person" to a different state of mind (think of what you've learned about the amygdala hijack) by using pauses and slowing down your voice while lowering your tone:

- "So, you feel that [repeat content]."
- "I want to make sure that I heard what you said: [repeat content]."
- "Are you saying that [repeat content]?"
- "If I heard you correctly, you [repeat content]."

Paraphrasing is also a helpful way to let the person know that you heard what he or she said before you responded. Effective paraphrasing repeats the essential content and major points of the person's statement.

After the Meeting

In order to help clarify your words and the answers you gave to questions during the meeting, it is always helpful to satisfy the "why" question that almost always lingers in the back of someone's mind. You want to fill in the blanks before someone does it for you:

- "During the meeting, my purpose for asking _____ was _____." (This answers the "why" question and goes a little deeper by giving a motivation statement as well.)

- "What I want you to know about my reasoning is
  _____." (This phrasing contains a multiple
  message: "There are some things I don't want you to know"
  or "There are some things you might not need to know").
- "It might be helpful for you to understand
  _____." (This also conveys that there
  is additional information that will help answer the
  "why" question.)

Habits for Better Leadership: Meeting Dos and Don'ts

This is not an exhaustive list by any means. Plus, this list keeps growing with every client interaction I have. It is simply a handy reminder.

Don'ts

- Don't interrupt people when they are talking.
- Don't tell people what they "should" do.
- Don't finish someone's sentence.
- Don't start a sentence with the words "Yes, but . . ." or "However."
- Don't look at your cell phone before or during a meeting.

Dos

- Do paraphrase as often as possible, but especially whenever someone is making a "point" or has expressed strong feelings.
- Do compliment and say "thank you."
- Do listen to connect.
- Do sit up, give eye contact, and smile.
- Do put your cell phone face down.

Personal Inventory Exercise

Day 1

- Today, pay attention to how many meetings you "need" to attend. Then set your intention for the meetings.
- What did you notice about yourself during the meeting?

Day 2

- Today, observe yourself during the meetings you attend. How did you sit? Where were your hands? Did you make good eye contact? Did you pay attention and join the discussion?
- What did you notice?

Day 3

- Today, if possible, see or hear how your coworkers are responding and interacting with others. For example, instead of looking at your cell phone before the meeting starts, ask open-ended questions of others.
- What did you see or hear?

Day 4

- Today, offer a "thank you" or express gratitude for either the accomplishments or the participation of those in attendance at meetings.
- What did you notice in response to your statements?

Day 5

- Today, during the meetings you attend, ask for someone's opinion, or ask a clarifying question about someone's statement.
- What did you find out?

TRY THIS

After every meeting, ask yourself how often you offered support and affirmation for the desired outcome for the meeting. Deconstruct any conversations you had before and after the meeting. What did you find out, and what are your conclusions about the conversations? Were they positive? Did they help to build trust, or did they promote self-interest?

CHAPTER 11

EMPATHY

The Most Essential
Leadership Skill

Empathy is the ability to recognize someone else's map of the world and understand his or her perspective. More and more research confirms that empathy is the number one skill necessary for effective leadership. (I say it goes hand in hand with good listening.)

From an emotional intelligence perspective, empathy is the ability to recognize, understand, and respect the feelings, thoughts, and actions of others. When leaders have the ability to see a situation from the viewpoint of another person and imagine what that person might be thinking or feeling, they have the ability to express empathy. Leaders can embody this style of empathetic leadership regardless of their personal or professional view of the other person. Being empathetic requires using the skills of emotional intelligence.

A recent study by the Center for Creative Leadership found that the ability to understand what others are feeling is a needed and effective skill set for leaders. The study concluded, "As managers hone their empathy skills through listening, perspective-taking, and compassion, they are improving their leadership effectiveness and increasing the chances of success in the job."[1] Dare I say that is the role of emotional intelligence? And its importance is growing as the modern work climate continues to change.

As I replay the conversations I have had with my clients, it's clear that the real struggle for most of them is trying to be an effective leader in the midst of monumental change and continual demands for improved productivity. In addition, leaders are required to be sensitive to the needs of staff while mediating real or potential conflicts. In order to be truly effective as a leader, you must be emotionally intelligent. There is no other way.

The real strength of an emotionally intelligent leader is the ability to be self-aware and to pinpoint the emotions of others. Yet being continually aware of our own emotions can be the most difficult task we perform on a daily basis. That is the point of the daily exercises provided with every chapter of this book.

Some leaders might say that it is next to impossible to be totally self-aware. Although this might be true, it becomes even more crucial for leaders to be aware of how their employees are feeling on a daily basis. Every effort toward becoming more emotionally intelligent makes a difference.

In 2011, the American Psychological Association reported that 49 percent of U.S. employees feel "undervalued" at work.[2] Another study, by the American Association of Critical Care Nurses, indicated that 77 percent of nurses and other critical care providers are concerned about disrespect—from verbal abuse to general rudeness and insults.[3] Yet only 7 percent of the 1,700 nurses, physicians, clinical-care staff, and administrators spoke up.

A similar study in 2010 found that 85 percent of nurses work with people who demonstrate disrespect (e.g., yelling, shouting, swearing, and name calling).[4] This treatment undercuts others' respect for the nurses' professional opinion and makes it much harder for them to do their job. Twenty percent of the respondents were seriously considering leaving their job as a result. Yet only 35 percent of the nurse managers reported that they had spoken up to the person whose disrespect had caused the greatest negative impact.

It is interesting to note how few people in these studies spoke up to their manager or to the person whose behavior concerned them the most. An emotionally intelligent leader (and workplace) would recognize not just the need for some crucial conversations but also the lack of empathy and appreciation that is creating the issue in the first place.

Humans are emotional creatures. We might think we are ruled by logic, but as you can see, emotions are the name of the game. The more aware you become of your own, the more you realize what affects others, including your employees. A recent study in the United Kingdom looked at the work attitudes of 2,000 employees. The results of the study revealed that "eight out of ten people said they would turn down a big salary increase if it meant working with people they didn't like."[5]

Per this study, the top three things employees look for in a job are

- Responsibility
- Recognition
- Agreeable colleagues.

The top three things that keep employees in their current job are

- A good relationship with colleagues
- An enjoyable job role
- A good relationship with their boss.

These findings suggest that focusing on talent management and appreciation can produce a real return on investment. A little respect and appreciation go a long way toward employee happiness. Recognize that your staff is composed of emotional beings; the more you treat them as such, the more successful you will be.

Effective leaders have a deeper understanding of appreciation, and they do more than simply express their gratitude. The best leaders find a way to help people feel significant. Successful leaders know the meaning and impact of being empathetic. According to a LinkedIn article by *Forbes* contributor George Anders, the most important job skill for 2020 is empathy.[6]

The results from the Center for Creative Leadership study mentioned earlier clearly demonstrate that empathy is positively correlated with job performance.[7] The study also found that upper management viewed managers who showed more empathy toward their direct reports as better performers. In summary, the study found the following:

- Higher levels of empathy in managers produced higher effectiveness.
- Empathetic managers were seen as positive assets to the organization.
- Empathetic managers improved their leadership effectiveness.
- Empathetic managers increased job performance ratings by subordinates.

Although empathy is a skill that takes time to develop, it is probably one of the most underutilized. Emotionally intelligent leaders who practice reading the emotions of others and who respond appropriately with empathy are the most effective leaders in any organization.

Seven Effective Steps to Be an Empathetic Leader

1. **Preprogram**. Before a meeting or conversation, pre-program yourself about what you want to say and how you want to say it (e.g., "How do I want to present myself?").

2. **Listen**. For the most part . . . simply listen! Ask clarifying questions when necessary (e.g., "Are you also saying that _____ ?").

3. **Reflect**. Replay the conversation by using paraphrasing to reflect back the feelings you heard the other person express (e.g., "So you are feeling like no one cares as much as you do?").

4. **Ask questions**. Ask clarifying questions about any generalizations, deletions, or distortions to make sure you understand what the other person is thinking and feeling (e.g., "Are you saying that *everyone* in the organization does this?").

5. **Stand in their shoes**. If you are helping to resolve a conflict, invite your employee to better understand the opposing perspective by helping him or her to see how the other person might be feeling (e.g., "How do you think _____ might be feeling right now?").

6. **Review**. After a meeting or conversation, review what you observed and learned from the conversation (e.g., "How could I have been more supportive and helpful?").

7. **Follow up**. As soon as appropriate, initiate another conversation with the same person, and revisit your previous conversation by asking caring questions (e.g., "I am wondering how you are feeling today about what we talked about last week?").

Personal Inventory Exercise

Day 1

- Today, when people share about their personal or professional life, notice their emotional state. For example, are they speaking louder, faster, or more intensely than usual?
- What did you discover?

Day 2

- Today, focus on asking clarifying questions when people share about their personal or professional life (e.g., "What do you mean when you say _____?").
- What did you notice?

Day 3

- Today, notice the "feeling words" people use to share about their personal or professional life. Reflect their feeling words back to them (e.g., "It sounds like you are frustrated").
- What did you notice?

Day 4

- Today, observe the nonverbal body language people use when sharing about their personal or professional life. Try subtly matching the body language, if possible.
- What did you observe?

Day 5

- Today, if people share about a problem or conflict in their personal or professional life, ask them to imagine how the other person might be feeling (e.g., "How do you think ____ might be feeling about _____?").
- What did you notice?

TRY THIS

The purpose of empathy is to convey to the other person that we really understand how he or she might be feeling. The other person doesn't need to share everything in great detail. In fact, we might not need to reflect every detail back to the other person. However, we can go deeper by reflecting a more compelling understanding (e.g., "When you really get to know how _____ is feeling, then you will start to allow the necessary changes in your relationship").

CHAPTER 12

MINDSET

The Most Critical Factor in Success

One of the reasons people seek a coach is because someone demanded that they improve some aspects of their leadership and interpersonal behavior, or else risk losing their job. As an executive coach, I often hear, "I don't know how," or "I just don't think I am cut out for this job." And my personal favorite, "I wish someone would simply tell me what to do." Unfortunately, these common statements say less about people's actual performance on the job, and more about what they believe about themselves—that is, their mindset.

Dr. Carol Dweck, one of the world's leading researchers in the field of motivation, outlined in her book *Mindset* how people's beliefs about themselves determine their success.[1] For decades, Dweck has been studying why some people succeed, whereas other people who are equally talented do not. She discovered that the one crucial determining factor is a person's mindset. In her words, "We now know that the growth mindset has a key role to play in helping us fulfill our mission and in helping *them* fulfill their potential."[2]

Not too long ago, I asked one of my clients how she became a successful CEO. Her reply: "It is simple, really. Being a successful leader begins with believing that you can do it." She had never heard of Carol Dweck's work, but she was practicing what Dweck calls a "growth mindset."

Whenever I share with my clients the basic understanding and importance of mindset, a whole new world of self-awareness opens up for them. A former client of mine who worked for a major company told me that among the many tools I gave his company for improving their business culture, having a growth mindset was the most important. The company now uses the growth mindset principle in its hiring practices and in how it treats its employees. In my client's words, "We now foster a growth mindset, and we teach our employees that they are ultimately in charge of their mind and their success as long as they are our employees."

Beginning with her research with children, Dr. Dweck found that success is based on the two ways that people think about learning.[3] She describes people as learning either from a fixed mindset or a growth mindset. The basic difference between the two mindsets is what people believe about themselves. People with a fixed mindset believe that one's potential success is limited or fixed from birth. Those with a growth mindset believe that skills and intelligence can be grown, improved on, and developed. The fixed mindset believes that we are not in control of our abilities, whereas the growth mindset asserts that we are.

One of the most important aspects of a growth mindset is a belief that our intelligence can be developed. People with a growth mindset believe in themselves and what they want to accomplish and share with the world. I have observed among my clients that when such a strong belief exists, people are capable of accomplishing whatever they want, and virtually no one and nothing can stop them.

Terry, a successful businesswoman I worked with, put it this way: "I have always held the belief that I can accomplish anything, and I owe that belief to my parents. They not only gave me opportunities to try things and fail, they gave me the mindset that a mistake is only good feedback to try again."

Not every client can describe where his or her perseverance came from, but many now understand what it takes to be successful. One client stated, "I learned a long time ago not to let any negative self-talk influence the positive belief I have in myself. I have a strong sense of who I am and how I want my employees to see me."

In line with Dweck's research, I have found that people with a growth mindset enjoy a challenge, and they embrace learning as if it were a daily vitamin. One client said it this way: "If you were to tell me when I graduated that I would end up as the CEO with a budget of billions of dollars, I probably would have asked you what you were smoking." Quoting Alfred Binet, the inventor of the IQ test, Dweck writes in *Mindset,* "It's not always the people who start out the smartest who end up the smartest."[4]

A key element of the belief system of people with a growth mindset is the knowledge that they can continue to grow through learning and experimenting. This helps them maintain a sheer determination for positive outcomes, even when faced with great challenges. A distinguishing characteristic of people with a growth mindset is the understanding that there are always new opportunities for learning and for changing the way an organization performs. You don't have to be born with a growth mindset. You can develop it, starting now.

Benefits of a Being a Growth Mindset Leader

The benefits of having a growth mindset as a leader include having devoted employees, receiving useful feedback, creating a culture of respect, and more. In particular, the benefits include the following.

- **Devoted employees.** A leader who expresses and finds inspiration from the thoughts and successes of others promotes higher retention and more motivated employees.
- **Failure is feedback.** A leader who sees failure as feedback

communicates the idea that we can learn from mistakes, which improves employee success and self-confidence.

- **Ready to learn.** A leader who wants to learn from others by co-creating solutions promotes self-esteem and a higher self-regard among his or her employees.
- **Respect for others.** A leader who recognizes individual growth and the quality of work creates a culture of respect and appreciation for differences.
- **Open to change.** A leader who is willing to take calculated risks indicates a willingness to learn and grow with change.

Benefits of a Growth Mindset Organization

The growth mindset offers the following benefits to the organization: an ability to self-correct, embrace challenges, work as a team, and more. In particular, the benefits include the following.

- **Allows for the press to stop.** A periodic and critical evaluation of how and why things are done helps organizations look at the potential risks and benefits of what they do. In the words of Carol Dweck, "A company that cannot self-correct cannot thrive."[5]
- **Embraces challenges.** Employees move toward finding solutions instead of avoiding problems, getting defensive, or simply giving up. Again, per Carol Dweck, "Educate [yourself] in the new growth mindset ways that . . . can support you: in taking on challenges and sticking to them,

bouncing back from failure, and helping and supporting others to grow."[6]

- **Cultivates a rapid response.** Companies with a growth mindset act on new ideas and discoveries more quickly, because any result (positive or negative) is feedback. As Dweck wrote, "Genius is not enough; we need to get the job done."[7]

- **Provides a teamwork approach.** Employees are encouraged to co-create and work as a team to find solutions. Dweck states, "The growth mindset allows people to value what they're doing regardless of the outcome."[8]

- **Produces devoted employees.** A company that expresses and finds inspiration from the thoughts and success of others promotes higher retention and more motivated employees. To quote Carol Dweck, people "admire effort, for, no matter what your ability is, effort is what ignites that ability and turns it into accomplishment."[9]

How to Move From a Fixed Mindset to a Growth Mindset

1. Cultivate a growth mindset for lifelong learning.

- From: "You will be a failure if you do it."
- To: "Many successful people had lots of failures before their successes."

2. **Recognize a growth mindset for changing strategies.**

- From: "I give up."
- To: "I can use a different approach to see how things change."

3. **Cultivate a growth mindset of what's possible.**

- From: "You can't do that, and you know it."
- To: "I'm not sure I can do it, but I think I can learn how."

4. **Develop a growth mindset of new beliefs.**

- From: "I never seem able to be organized."
- To: "In the past, I was not good at being organized, but I am now learning how to be good at it."

5. **Embrace a growth mindset of "not yet."**

- From: "I don't know how to do Sudoku puzzles."
- To: "I haven't learned how to do Sudoku puzzles *yet*."

What separates the average leader from the really successful leader is the ability to understand and adapt a growth mindset. It's clear from the research of Dweck and others that our mental attitude determines how we interpret and respond to life's situations. The two types of mindset give us a framework to better understand our map of the world. Our mindset matters in virtually every aspect of our lives.

Dweck's research teaches us that we can shift our mindset about what we believe about any limitations from our past. By moving from a fixed to a growth mindset, we can dramatically alter our professional success. Our mindset matters.

Personal Inventory Exercise

Day 1

- Today, notice that "fixed mindset" statements are an interpretation of how things have always been and an assertion that nothing will change.
- What did you notice about yourself and others?

Day 2

- Today, observe your self-talk. What did you notice about your inner dialogue? Did it reveal a fixed mindset or growth mindset?
- What did you notice?

Day 3

- Today, use growth mindset statements in at least three conversations. Pay attention to how people respond.
- What did you see or hear from others?

Day 4

- Today, use the words *yet* or *not yet* after you describe what you believe about yourself and your abilities.
- What did you find out about what you felt after adding *yet* or *not yet*?

Day 5

- Today, take ownership of your growth mindset, and only speak from a growth mindset.
- What did you find out?

TRY THIS

Pay even closer attention to your self-worth by using either a mixed mindset or a growth mindset to solve problems. For extra points, figure out what the benefits are for using a mixed mindset or a growth mindset throughout the day.

CHAPTER 13

THE SCARF MODEL

Building a Sense of Warmth and Security

We've covered a lot of ground in a short time, and you have sufficient information now to interact differently both at work and in your personal life. You now have the tools for increased self-awareness, to see the larger picture of how you relate to others, how they relate to you, and how the people around you relate to each other. I trust this primer will serve you well and be the basis for continued growth. Just like your intellectual intelligence has the capacity to expand, so does your emotional intelligence.

To help my clients understand the true drivers of human social behavior, I teach them about SCARF, a brain-based model for collaborating with and influencing others developed by David Rock, a neurologist and leadership coach. According to Rock, there are five domains that activate either the primary reward or the primary threat circuitry of the brain: status, certainty, autonomy, relatedness, and fairness. These are the key elements of the SCARF model.[1]

The SCARF principle represents the likelihood that the brain will tag an experience as good (reward) or bad (threat). As it scans the environment, the brain assesses the stimuli it encounters according to an "approach" or "avoid" survival mechanism. This mechanism is triggered by the amygdala, which has a tendency to generalize and overreact to often-inaccurate information. (This reaction is the amygdala hijack we discussed in Chapter 8.) You can implement this model as part of your emotional intelligence foundation. As one of my clients told me, "After you shared the SCARF model, I had it laminated, and I keep it with me all of the time." Another leader told me that she set it as her screen saver as a reminder about the importance of rewards for her staff.

Status

The first domain in the SCARF model, status, is about your relative importance to others—your place in the pecking order, your seniority at work, your relative position in a community, or your importance in a professional group or social club. If you are asked to join the boss for happy hour, for example, you might feel a significant boost in your status domain.

Threats

A perceived threat to one's status lights up the same part of the brain as a threat to one's life. A reduction in status resulting from being left out of an activity activates the same regions of the brain as physical pain. Rock even suggests taking a Tylenol at such times.[2] Some status threats include advice, instructions, or the suggestion that you might be slightly ineffective at your job. For some people, the question, "Can I offer you some feedback?" generates a similar response to hearing fast footsteps behind you at night.[3]

Rewards

People's sense of status can go up when they feel they are learning and improving and when other people pay attention to the improvement. Your status goes up when you beat your own best time at a task or sporting event or when you receive positive feedback, especially in public. One study showed that status increases when the boss simply smiles at you. Another study found that a boost in status felt similar to a financial windfall.[4]

Certainty

Certainty concerns being able to predict the future. According to Rock, the brain is prewired for certainty and is constantly trying to predict the near future. Without this certainty, the brain must draw on new data, using more resources and energy. A sense of certainty is rewarding, and examples are everywhere.

When you go to a Burger King for a Whopper, for instance, you know ahead of time what it is going to look like and taste like. There's a certain sense of comfort and relief in that knowledge. If you have ever returned to a place you have traveled to often and know well, you likely felt happiness and security because you could easily recall your mental maps.

Threats

There are small and large uncertainties all around us. Any kind of significant change generates uncertainty. If you sense that someone is not being transparent or not telling the truth, you will develop a small amount of uncertainty. Uncertainty can be reduced, for example, when you break down complex problems into smaller chunks. In other words, you don't need to eat the entire elephant at one time.

Rewards

Developing clear expectations for desired outcomes helps to decrease uncertainty. For example, tell people what to expect in the future (big picture), provide specific data about the change ahead, and tell them what you are going to do before you do it. Even telling a group that the meeting will start and end on time increases certainty.

Autonomy

Autonomy provides a sense of control (or choices) over events. A sense of not having autonomy can turn small stresses into an overwhelming stress. Having some control or even the illusion of choices increases the perception of autonomy. Autonomy is highly connected to the sense of efficacy and the ability to produce our desired outcome.

Threats

A sense of decreased or no autonomy is perceived as a threat. Taking away control or increasing oversight and accountability heightens the threat. Micromanaging can be seen as a threat to autonomy.

Rewards

Granting autonomy is seen as a reward—both an internal reward and an external reward. An external reward is something that someone gives us (e.g., a trophy), whereas an internal reward is something we feel inside (e.g., a sense of achievement). Providing people the opportunity for greater choice about what they do and when they do it increases rewards. Autonomy can be difficult in many organizations; however, rewards can include allowing employees to set up their desk as they like, take breaks when needed, manage their work hours, and organize their work flow.

Relatedness

Relatedness is a sense of safety with others. It involves a decision about who is "in" and who is "out"—or perhaps another way of saying it is, "Are you a friend or foe?" People naturally like to form "tribes" where they experience a sense of belonging. Even in large organizations, people develop small groups. In some cases, small-group formations are almost automatic. The next time you attend a conference, notice how people tend to sit in the same place during each session, surrounded by the same people. This relatedness gives people a feeling of safety.

Threats

People like to have a sense that they belong to something worthwhile, and, for the most part, they like to fit in and be part of a community. However, in most groups, people are put through a filter to separate those who are "like us" from those who are "our foes." Relatedness boils down to trust (i.e., "Do I trust you to be in my group?"). If people do not feel welcomed or included as part of a group, they most likely will have a decreased sense of belonging and relatedness.

Rewards

The more people trust one another, the stronger is their collaboration, and the more information is shared among people, groups, and teams. Increasing relatedness diminishes the foe response and increases trust within an organization. When people have a sense of being connected with others, they are more likely to feel greater trust and empathy toward others.[5]

Fairness

Fairness is a perception that one is treated fairly when compared with others. Many organizations use their policies and procedures to communicate a sense of fairness and equitable treatment of employees. However, fairness may be increased or decreased depending on the consistencies of interpretation and the implementation of policies and procedures.

Threats

A sense of unfairness can be triggered quite easily. As leaders, we can decrease the threat of perceived unfairness by being more transparent, increasing the level of communication, establishing clear expectations in all situations, allowing teams to develop their own rules (e.g., about cell phone use), and seeing things through the other person's eyes (i.e., practicing empathy).

Rewards

Employees' sense of fairness is increased when clear guidelines and procedures are followed in a consistent manner. People who perceive others as unfair might not feel empathy for their pain, and, in some cases, they might feel rewarded when others are punished for not following policies and procedures. The important thing to remember is that the *perception* of fairness is often the key. In other words, when it comes to fairness, the reality may matter less than how a person perceives reality. Research has shown that even when fair and unfair offers are made equally valuable, people are happier to receive fair offers than unfair ones.[6]

SCARF in Action

Status: "I am so glad to have you as a member of this team."

Certainty: "We will begin the meeting at 8 a.m. and be finished before noon."

Autonomy: "Feel free to delete anything on the list that doesn't belong there or add anything that is missing."

Relatedness: "We are wondering if you want to join us for lunch today."

Fairness: "There are clear procedures in place for how we will respond."

If it is true that emotions drive people and people drive outcomes, then being aware and using the SCARF model almost guarantees positive outcomes. One leader I worked with described the SCARF model as the best management idea in his twenty years of being the CEO. I agree.

Personal Inventory Exercise

Day 1

- Today, pay attention to status threats and rewards and how they present themselves.
- What did you notice about threats to someone's status? What did you notice about the rewards to someone's status?

Day 2

- Today, pay attention to certainty threats and rewards and how they present themselves.
- What did you notice about threats to someone's certainty? What did you notice about rewards to someone's certainty?

Day 3

- Today, pay attention to autonomy threats and rewards and how they present themselves.
- What did you notice about threats to someone's autonomy? What did you notice about the rewards to someone's autonomy?

Day 4

- Today, pay attention to relatedness threats and rewards and how they present themselves.
- What did you notice about threats to someone's

relatedness? What did you notice about the rewards to someone's relatedness?

Day 5

- Today, pay attention to fairness threats and rewards and how they present themselves.
- What did you notice about threats to someone's fairness? What did you notice about the rewards to someone's fairness?

TRY THIS

At the end of the day, journal the ways you helped increase the rewards of the SCARF model that day. What can you do to increase the rewards even more? Focus on each letter of the SCARF model, and create one goal for each letter per day.

CONCLUSION
Time For Action

Y ou've worked your way through the lessons in this book, completing the daily exercises and building your self-awareness. Now it's time to take those tools for a first drive around the block.

What makes some leaders more effective than others is not what they do but what they do *not* do. Conventional wisdom teaches us to develop more and more strategies to help us better manage others, yet sometimes less is more. Emotional intelligence is not a strategy or another item to add to your already crowded to-do list. The whole goal of emotional intelligence is to be able to get through every day knowing that you did the best you could. You get better every day.

A client once asked me, "I hate to say it this way, but how can we better manipulate others to do what we want them to do?" Emotional intelligence—and leadership, for that matter—is not about manipulation. It's about real empathy. It's relating to each other's human needs, and knowing yourself.

Many leaders wish there were a magic pill to give employees to get them to do what needs to be done. There are plenty of books offering wisdom, tactics, and strategies along these lines, some claiming to have the silver bullet or the secret trick that works every time. The real key, though, is knowing which strategy is needed when. Strategies and interventions only work if used in the proper context and in the appropriate way. How do you know what and when that may be? By tuning in to your emotional intelligence.

My work is all about helping people be better equipped to meet leadership challenges. It's easier to become an emotionally intelligent leader when you have the background knowledge you need (the knowledge you've gained from reading this book), along with the tools to use (your Leader's Toolbox follows in the Appendix). My clients are often relieved to know that they can get better results *without* adding one more thing to their bag of tricks. Knowing what to let go of is equally as essential as knowing what to implement. Letting go of stress and worry is important. You can take your team and organization to greater heights by relaxing the need to control and by trusting the process.

My clients have found this primer and the Leadership Toolbox to be helpful in their daily management of employees. I trust you will, as well. Now that you know the basics of emotional intelligence, you can't "unknow" them, and you will go forward making better decisions with newfound awareness.

The benefits of being an emotionally intelligent leader are endless. You are now able to be the difference that makes the difference. And for that, I thank you. You will see the change that occurs in your organization. Besides that, you'll sleep better at night. That's more than worth the effort it took to get you here.

As you immerse yourself in your newfound emotional intelligence skills, you will be happy to see how much more gets done and how effective and productive *everyone* can be when the dynamics shift. Is emotional intelligence the magic bullet? No, but it sure works magic. Try it and you will see for yourself. That's all the proof you need.

APPENDIX

The Leader's Toolbox

Consider the information in this primer as tools in your emotional intelligence toolbox. As you begin to implement them, you might find that you forget to reach for them while in the "heat of battle." No worries. As you continue to work with your new set of tools, you will incorporate more and more of them into your leadership skill set without having to actively think about what you are doing. They will become part of your "muscle memory."

The purpose of this appendix is to provide a quick reference guide for how and when to use specific emotional intelligence tools in a given situation. Most tools in the toolbox begin with self-awareness. I cannot state enough that self-awareness is key to being a successful leader. For you to be a more effective and more influential leader, your solution to every situation—before any action is taken—must begin with your own self-awareness audit. Begin by asking the right questions in order to effect the best results.

Boundaries

Self-Awareness Audit

- Was a personal or workplace boundary violated, and, if so, by whom (e.g., inappropriate touching or the inappropriate sharing of information, on Facebook or in conversation)?
- Was a clear and appropriate boundary already in place? Was the boundary formal or informal, verbal or unspoken, written or assumed?
- How was the boundary communicated to all parties concerned?

Course of Action

- Decide what boundary was violated and by whom.
- Share how the boundary (whether formal or informal, personal or workplace) can be better communicated without ambiguity and misinterpretation.
- Clarify how workplace and professional boundaries are consistent with workplace policies, procedures, and guidelines.

Example

Leslie was promoted to chief operating officer (COO) from an executive position. While she was an executive, she maintained her close friendship ties from more than fifteen years at the company. She and her good friends went out for drinks after work, and they even shared family vacations together. Nothing was off limits, including discussions about the company and other employees. When Leslie and her friends were together, everyone freely shared what they thought about the CEO and other top management.

Even before becoming the COO, Leslie felt awkward when conversations drifted to what was wrong with everyone else in the company. Intuitively, Leslie knew that she needed to make a change in her "BFF" relationships. With the help of coaching, Leslie began to evaluate what were appropriate and inappropriate conversations with her friends. She started to set boundaries by not going out to drink on Fridays and not getting together every weekend with families connected to the company.

Leslie also decided to state what her future boundaries would look like with her friends—for example, absolutely no discussion about work and work colleagues. She believed her relationships had to change if she were to be viewed by everyone in the company as an effective, professional COO.

Unfortunately, when she put these boundaries in place, Leslie found out that her friendships were almost entirely based on company gossip and innuendos. Soon the old friendships faded to a more professional level at work, and the outside gatherings faded away. Any new relationships she formed at work followed Leslie's new boundaries and self-understanding as COO.

Amygdala Hijack

Self-Awareness Audit

- What has happened both physically and emotionally (e.g., what was said, what was the tone of voice, and what non-verbal communication did you observe?)?
- What were the triggers for the hijack?
- What is the emotional damage and possible fallout from the hijack?

Course of Action

- Decide to embrace the obvious "elephant in the room" as an amygdala hijack.
- Acknowledge that the hijack took place, and agree that all parties will behave better next time.
- Analyze the triggers and how to avoid them in the future.

Example

Bob was one of the managers at a large corporation. He had a history of angry outbursts whenever anyone tried to contradict his ideas about how things should be done. His eyes would narrow, and he would get red in the face before verbally lashing out at someone for being an idiot. No one dared confront Bob about his behavior, because he responded with verbal putdowns, treating people like children. His CEO said that Bob needed to change and get better control of his anger or he would lose his job.

Although Bob was forced to seek out coaching, he was aware

of his anger issues and how they affected his coworkers and family members. In Bob's words, "I feel helpless when my anger starts to get out of control. And sometimes it takes hours for me to cool off."

Bob began his pilgrimage toward better self-control with self-awareness. He was able to name his triggers, and he soon learned different ways to respond. A major breakthrough was the result of education about the amygdala hijack and how neurochemicals work in the brain. Bob learned new coping skills, such as focused breathing, and gained an ability to recognize his triggers before an amygdala hijack took place.

Parent/Adult–Child Interactions

Self-Awareness Audit

- How are you feeling, and what are your emotions (e.g., do you feel like a child?)?
- When in the past did you feel a similar emotion?
- What was the tipping point or the trigger (e.g., was it the person's voice, body language, or words used—e.g., "You always _____"?)?

Course of Action

- Clarify whether the trigger is current or from another time in your personal history.
- Decide how, in the future, you can respond as an "adult," not as a "parent" or "child."
- Respond by paraphrasing and by asking a clarifying question before making a statement.

Example

Cindy holds a degree in psychology, and she understands the concept of transactional analysis and how it works. Cindy knows when she is being talked to as a child or when someone else is "parenting" her. In fact, when talking to coworkers, she might even say something like, "I don't want to parent you, but I think you might want to consider something else."

Cindy is very self-aware, and she has learned how to recognize when she feels like someone is treating her like a child by parenting her behavior. What Cindy hasn't learned is how to respond without disgust.

As the result of coaching, Cindy found out that almost all of her triggers could be traced back to her childhood and into young adulthood. Her parents had a difficult time giving her independence, and they treated her like a child well into her teenage years. Whenever someone at work told her what to do, Cindy reverted back to her default emotional response, formed when she lived at home with her parents. Cindy now has a larger toolbox of responses for when she wants to parent someone or when someone else treats her like a child.

Self–Talk

Self-Awareness Audit

- What do I hear from my self-talk?
- Is my self-talk negative or positive, fair or unfair, real or imagined?
- When and how often does my self-talk distract or hijack my positive self-image?

Course of Action

- Edit what you hear, and then create a new, positive self-talk script.
- Focus on your positive accomplishments, and remind your brain about the truth.
- Practice positive self-talk every single day.

Example

Ann has been carrying around an inner voice for years. The voice reminds her that she is never good enough and that nothing she does will ever be successful, including her marriage. At one coaching session, Ann said, "I would never allow someone else to talk to me the way I allow my self-talk. I would probably slap them in the face."

Ann learned to edit her self-talk through an inner dialogue of correction and counter self-impressions. She was coached about the dangers of negative self-talk. She learned what positive self-talk sounds like and how to use it more often.

By incorporating a positive self-talk approach, Ann began to rewire her brain with affirmations and positive thoughts. She practiced positive self-talk every day without fail. Not only did she notice that her words in conversations were more positive, her friends noticed as well. One person said, "It is almost like you changed your personality."

Multiple Messages

Self-Awareness Audit

- What are my (and others') multiple messages?
- What might be the intended message?
- Which message do I hear, and which message do others hear?

Course of Action

- Listen to connect; ask clarifying questions about your assumptions.
- Share what you heard, and ask whether what you heard is the intended message.
- Allow time for the other person to agree, deny, or resend his or her intended message.

Example

Stan is a manager who reports to one director and oversees one hundred fifty employees. Stan likes to describe his job by saying, "All day long, either I am telling someone what to do or someone is telling me what to do." He calls himself a "functional schizophrenic" who tries not to make assumptions about what others are saying.

When Stan learned to listen for multiple messages, he found himself better able to manage others and respond to his boss. He told me, "I have stopped assuming what others are saying and started asking clarifying questions instead. My life is much better." Stan found out how effective paraphrasing and asking questions can be in making others more accountable for what they say.

Preprogram

Self–Awareness Audit

- How do I see myself in the situation before me (e.g., what is my posture?)?
- What is my anxiety, and can I reframe it with words (e.g., "I am excited to _____")?
- What is my positive self-talk, and what will I edit from any negative self-talk?

Course of Action

- Practice what you want to say and how you want to say it.
- Before every meeting, practice the akimbo stance (hands on hips; the Wonder Woman stance).
- Take three very deep breaths from the diaphragm before any meeting and before speaking.

Example

Robert is a new CEO who does not yet feel very confident in his role. Robert keeps a hectic schedule, which probably will never change as long as he is the CEO. All day long, he moves from one meeting to the next and one phone call to the next. When I first started coaching Robert, he expressed his need for coaching by saying, "I simply want to catch my breath and be better prepared throughout the day."

After Robert started using some basic breathing techniques and after he gave more intentional thought to how he wanted to represent himself, things started to change. Before and during many of his meetings, Robert intentionally used his focused breathing to present a calmer demeanor. He also visualized himself in the meeting (e.g., where and how he was going to sit). Using the akimbo stance before his more intense meetings, Robert started to gain more self-confidence, and he became more comfortable in his role as CEO.

Triangles

Self-Awareness Audit

- Who is being triangled? With whom (e.g., the administration, another employee)? How many people are included in the triangle?
- What is causing the triangle (e.g., fear, anxiety, anger, jealousy)?
- What is the positive intention of the triangle?

Course of Action

- Listen without condemnation, and paraphrase as much as possible.
- Listen for deletions, generalizations, and distortions. Then ask clarifying questions (e.g., "How do you know _____? What tells you _____ ?").
- De-triangle by sharing the information collaboratively. Then objectively respond to the concerns expressed in the triangle by analyzing whether the energy of the triangle matches the intensity of the anxiety.

Example

Loraine can see and feel when a triangle is occurring better than anyone I know. She saw how destructive triangles could be in relationships, and she noticed that the triangles increased with the increased anxiety in her department. Loraine knew how to help her staff de-triangle. Her process, which follows, can also help you and your staff.

How to De-Triangle and Solve Problems With Staff

1. **Listen to the problem.** It is important that staff be heard by management. The best way to let someone know he or she has been heard is by paraphrasing what was spoken. Paraphrasing—or restating in your own words what someone said—is a form of empathic listening, or showing that we care.

2. **Ask for attempted solutions.** By asking what solutions someone has already attempted, we learn how he or she has viewed the problem. By continuing to ask clarifying questions, we learn what solutions or possible steps might have been overlooked.

3. **Brainstorm possible options.** The message we want to send to staff is that they have choices. Our main focus is to brainstorm with staff about what are the best choices available for the particular situation. There is no such thing as failure, only feedback.

4. **Agree on a course of action.** Maintaining emotional intelligence, openness, and sensitivity to our staff equips us to achieve the best course of action.

Example

Mary wants people to like her. In fact, being liked is her number one goal each and every day. She also believes that being a leader means that she has all of the answers. On most days, Mary does a great job, and people often come to her to solve problems they have with other workers. Mary listens and even paraphrases what she hears.

Unfortunately, Mary enjoys being triangled into the problems in her department. She told me, "I do like to solve problems, and I do a good job of listening. What I now know is that I am not helping my staff to at least make an attempt to solve the problem. I have also learned that I am not helping our succession plan if I am the only problem solver."

Emotional Intelligence Filter Questions

Answer the conversation questions: The questions below are good ones to ask yourself before speaking when you are being tri-angled about your impressions of someone else.

- "Is it true?"
- "Is it necessary"
- "Is it kind?"[1]

Answer the constructive criticism questions: These are good questions to answer when you feel an impulse to speak your mind.

- "Does this need to be said?"
- "Does this need to be said by me?"
- "Does this need to be said by me now?"[2]

Answer the Cartesian questions. These are good questions to answer when making a decision.

- "What will happen if we do _____?"
- "What will happen if we don't do _____?"
- "What won't happen if we do _____?"
- "What won't happen if we don't do _____?"

Example

Mark used to simply say whatever came to his mind. He made impulsive decisions, and whenever someone asked him how he felt, he did not mince his words. This was especially true when he was evaluating others who might not live up to his expectations.

With coaching and greater self-awareness, Mark learned to use the emotional intelligence filters on a regular basis. Mark describes it this way: "Hardly a day goes by that I don't use several of the filter questions. It has made a huge difference for what I say, either before or after a decision has been made."

Chapter Notes

Chapter 2

1   Business Wire. (2006, April 25). "Research by the Ken Blanchard Companies Reveals Critical Skills and Common Mistakes of Leaders, Key Traits That Make or Break Those at the Top" [press release]. Retrieved from http://www.businesswire.com/news/home/20060425005379/en/Research-Ken-Blanchard-Companies-Reveals-Critical-Skills.

Chapter 4

1   Reldan Nadler, *Leading With Emotional Intelligence: Hands-On Strategies for Building Confident and Collaborative Star Performers* (New York: McGraw Hill, 2011), p. 271.

2   Noam Chomsky, *Aspects of the Theory of Syntax* (Cambridge, MA: MIT Press, 1965), p. 145.

Chapter 5

1   Dan Ariely, *Predictably Irrational: The Hidden Forces That Shape Our Decisions* (New York: HarperCollins, 2009).

2   Daniel H. Pink, *Drive: The Surprising Truth About What Motivates Us* (New York: Riverhead Books, 2009).

3   Teresa Amabile and Steven Kramer, *The Progress Principle: Using Small Wins to Ignite Joy, Engagement, and Creativity at Work* (Boston: Harvard Business Review Press, 2011).

4   Teresa Amabile and Steven Kramer, *The Progress Principle*, p. 22.

Chapter 6

1   *Pirates of the Caribbean: The Curse of the Black Pearl* (film), directed by Gore Verbinski (Burbank, CA: Walt Disney Pictures, 2003).

2   Murray Bowen, *Family Therapy in Clinical Practice* (New York: Aronson, 1978).

Chapter 7

1   Edwin Friedman, *The Failure of Nerve: Leadership in the Age of the Quick Fix* (New York: Church, 2007).

2   Edwin Friedman, *The Failure of Nerve*, p. 183.

3   Murray Bowen, *Family Therapy in Clinical Practice* (New York: Aronson, 1978).

Chapter 8

1   Daniel Goleman, *Emotional Intelligence: Why It Can Matter More Than IQ* (New York: Bantam, 1995).

2   M. D. Lieberman et al. (2007). "Putting Feelings Into Words: Affect Labeling Disrupts Amygdala Activity to Affective Stimuli." *Psychological Science* 18 (2007): 421–428.

Chapter 9

1   Relly Nadler, "Why Emotional Intelligence?" Retrieved from True North Leadership: http://www.truenorthleadership.com/why-emotional-intelligence/.

2   Daniel Goleman, *Focus: The Hidden Driver of Excellence* (New York: HarperCollins, 2013).
E. Doman and S. Wolff, "Emotional Intelligence Competencies in the Team and Team Leader: A Multi-Level Examination of the Impact of Emotional Intelligence on Team Performance." *Journal of Management Development* 27, no. 1 (2008): 55–75.
Daniel Goleman, Richard Boyatzis, and Annie McKee, *Primal Leadership: Unleashing the Power of Emotional Intelligence* (Cambridge, MA: Harvard University Press, 2002).

3   Edwin Friedman, *The Failure of Nerve: Leadership in the Age of the Quick Fix* (New York: Church, 2007), p. 87.

4   Amy Cuddy, "Your Body Language May Shape Who You Are" (TED Talk, June 2012). Available at https://www.ted.com/talks/amy_cuddy_your_body_language_shapes_who_you_are.

5   Marco Iacoboni, *Mirroring People: The New Science of How We Connect With Others* (New York: Picador, 2008).

Chapter 10

1   David Rock, *Your Brain at Work: Strategies for Overcoming*

Distraction, Regaining Focus, and Working Smarter All Day Long
(New York: Harper, 2009).

2   National Center for Biotechnology Information. (2016). "Attention Span Statistics." Retrieved from Statistic Brain: http://www.
statisticbrain.com/attention-span-statistics/.

Chapter 11

1   Bill Gentry, "Empathy in the Workplace: A Tool for Effective Leadership" (white paper, Center for Creative Leadership, Greensboro,
NC, n.d.).

2   American Psychological Association. (2013, March 5). "APA
Survey Finds US Employers Unresponsive to Employee Needs"
(press release). Retrieved from http://www.apa.org/news/press/
releases/2013/03/employee-needs.aspx.

3   David Maxfield et al., "Silence Kills: The Seven Crucial Conversations for Healthcare" (report, American Association of Critical-
Care Nurses and VitalSmarts, 2005).

4   David Maxfield et al., "The Silent Treatment: Why Safety Tools
and Checklists Aren't Enough" (report, Patient Safety and Quality
Healthcare, Middleton, MA, 2011).

5   Association of Accounting Technicians. (2014, July 15).
"Britain's Workers Value Companionship and Recognition Over a Big Salary, a Recent Report Revealed." Retrieved
from   https://www.aat.org.uk/about-aat/press-releases/britains-
workers-value-companionship-recognition-over-big-salary.

6   George Anders, "The Number One Job Skill in 2020," *LinkedIn
Pulse,* June 11, 2012. Retrieved from https://www.linkedin.com/
pulse/20130611180041-59549-the-no-1-job-skill-in-2020.

7   Bill Gentry, "Empathy in the Workplace."

Chapter 12

1   Carol Dweck, *Mindset: The New Psychology of Success* (New York:
Random House, 2006).

2   Carol Dweck, *Mindset,* p. 221.

3   Carol Dweck, *Mindset.*

4   Carol Dweck, *Mindset,* p. 5.

5   Carol Dweck, *Mindset,* p. 109.

6　Carol Dweck, *Mindset,* p. 260.
7　Carol Dweck, *Mindset,* p. 130.
8　Carol Dweck, *Mindset,* p. 48.
9　Carol Dweck, *Mindset,* p. 41.

Chapter 13

1　David Rock and Al Ringleb, *Handbook of NeuroLeadership* (New York: Author, 2013).
2　David Rock, "Your Brain on Facebook," *Harvard Business Review*, May 18, 2012. Retrieved from https://hbr.org/2012/05/your-brain-on-facebook.
3　David Rock, "Learning About the Brain Changes Everything: David Rock at TEDxTokyo" (TED Talk, February 1, 2013). Retrieved from https://www.youtube.com/watch?v=uDIyxxayNig.
4　David Rock, "Learning About the Brain."
5　David Rock and Al Ringleb, *Handbook of NeuroLeadership.*
6　Golnaz Tabibnia, Ajay Satpute, and Matthew Liberman, "The Sunny Side of Fairness." *Psychological Science* 19, no. 4 (2008): 339–347.

Appendix

1　Mary Ann Pietzker, *Miscellaneous Poems* (London: Griffith and Farron, 1872), p. 54.
2　Craig Ferguson, *Does This Need to Be Said?* (comedy documentary, Production Partners, 2011).

About the Author

DR. DON BOOZ is the founder of Booz and Associates, Inc., an executive and organizational development firm. His clients often describe him as a conversational anthropologist, and he is recognized for his expertise in linking emotional intelligence to personal and professional goals. Known as one of the top executive coaches in the Kansas City area, Don has been awarded the Professional Certified Coach designation by the International Coaching Federation.

Using an action-oriented approach, Don teaches emotional intelligence and leadership skills to organizations, including The University of Kansas Health System. He is educated as a marriage and family therapist, executive coach, Conversational Intelligence™ Coach, and Master Practitioner in Neuro Linguistic Programming. A keynote speaker, Don is also a trainer for Jack Canfield, conducting workshops for increasing personal and professional success in today's world.

Don is one of a few in this world who teaches individuals and organizations how to improve their Conversational Intelligence. Don works with a variety of individuals and organizations but, in his words, "I most enjoy working with leaders who want to be 'The difference that makes the difference.'"

www.ingramcontent.com/pod-product-compliance
Lightning Source LLC
Chambersburg PA
CBHW050107210326
41519CB00015BA/3855

Carbon-Based Nanocarriers for Drug Delivery

Carbon-Based Nanocarriers for Drug Delivery enlists the latitudes and advancements in the synthesis processes, functionalization, and applications of carbon-based nanomaterials (CBNs) in targeted drug delivery systems (DDSs). It covers the applicability and suitability of CBNs as nanocarriers for efficient drug delivery application via elucidating the recent advancements in CBNs, their functionalized and innovative derivatives, and the relevant case studies. The book explores the necessity, efficacy, toxicological aspects, and challenges for the application of CBN in targeted DDSs. Some of the features of this book are as follows:

- Provides elaborative description on significance and adaptability of carbon-based nanomaterial in targeted drug delivery for wide ranges of therapeutics.
- Delivers a full-spectrum discussion on drug delivery through carbon-based nanocarriers.
- Explores each carbon-based nanocarrier fundamentally for its drug- and gene-delivery-related applications.
- Describes critical discussion on various toxicological effects over the utilization of these nanocarriers.
- Embraces existing as well as novel technologies/methodologies related to the synthesis and functionalization of CBNs, including graphene, graphene oxide, carbon quantum dots, carbon nanotube, fullerene, and smart carbon-based nanocarriers.

This book is aimed at researchers and graduate students in materials and pharmaceutical engineering, including drug delivery systems.